THE LIFE-HISTORY OF BRITISH LIZARDS

AND THEIR LOCAL DISTRIBUTION IN THE BRITISH ISLES

BY

GERALD R. LEIGHTON, M.D., F.R.S.E.

AUTHOR OF "BRITISH SERPENTS"
EDITOR OF "THE FIELD NATURALIST'S QUARTERLY" ETC. ETC.
INTERIM PROFESSOR OF PATHOLOGY, ROYAL (DICK) VETERINARY COLLEGE, EDINBURGH

EDINBURGH:
GEORGE A. MORTON, 42 GEORGE STREET
LONDON: SIMPKIN, MARSHALL, & CO. LTD.
1903

In the interest of creating a more extensive selection of rare historical book reprints, we have chosen to reproduce this title even though it may possibly have occasional imperfections such as missing and blurred pages, missing text, poor pictures, markings, dark backgrounds and other reproduction issues beyond our control. Because this work is culturally important, we have made it available as a part of our commitment to protecting, preserving and promoting the world's literature. Thank you for your understanding.

TO THE

FIELD NATURALISTS

OF THE

BRITISH ISLES

PREFACE

Two years ago, in 1901, when I published my book on *British Serpents*, a kindly critic was good enough to say that the only fault he had to find with that book was that it did not deal with the lizards as well. I am only too conscious that there were many other faults in that book, but I have in this present work endeavoured to remove the one indicated. This book is intended as a companion volume to the first; the two together completing the account of all the British reptiles, snakes and lizards, from the point of view of the field naturalist.

The plan adopted here is much the same as that in the former book. For the reports on the distribution of lizards in special districts that are given I am indebted to those workers whose names are given under each district.

In writing this book I have tried to keep in mind that the field naturalist should, in his study of a special group of animals, become well acquainted with their relationships to the animals most nearly connected to them, and also should have a clear idea of all that is involved in the study of one group, whether he intends to study all aspects or not. I have therefore included, in a modified form, the Introduction which I wrote for the series of articles on "British Field Zoology" now appearing in *The Field Naturalist's Quarterly*. It forms the first chapter of this book. For the same reason the special subjects towards the end of Part I. of the volume are dealt with, as it seemed to me that any description of our lizards would be incomplete without them. One or two matters, such as Hibernation and Sloughing, which were fully described in my book on the snakes, are now touched upon more briefly.

The great majority of the illustrations are by Mr. Douglas English, taken from living lizards by the "control method." One or two are from photographs of my own; and that of the female slow-worm and her young is by Rev. Cornish Watkins. This latter appeared in *The Field Naturalist's Quarterly* for August 1902. The diagrams I am personally responsible for. The outline drawings of the heads of the various species have been drawn for this work by Dr. O. Charnock Bradley, F.R.S.E., to whom I am much indebted. I have also to thank G. A. Boulenger, F.R.S., for his ever-ready advice and much valuable assistance.

The chapter on the anatomy of a lizard is based upon the description given in Professor Parker's

Zootomy, to which readers who wish greater detail are referred. For many other facts I am indebted to Dr. Hans Gadow's *Amphibia and Reptiles*, a work which all reptile students should possess.

Lastly, I have to thank numerous field-naturalist correspondents in various parts of the country for their assistance and information.

GERALD LEIGHTON.

17 HARTINGTON PLACE, EDINBURGH,
November 1903.

CONTENTS

PART I

CHAP.		PAGE
I.	INTRODUCTORY	1
II.	THE ORDER LACERTILIA	8
III.	THE ANATOMY OF THE LIZARDS	14
IV.	THE SLOW-WORM, *Anguis fragilis*	24
V.	THE SLOW-WORM—*continued*	37
VI.	THE COMMON LIZARD, *Lacerta vivipara*	45
VII.	THE SAND LIZARD, *Lacerta agilis*	55
VIII.	THE GREEN LIZARD, *Lacerta viridis*	68
IX.	THE WALL LIZARD, *Lacerta muralis*	76
X.	THE SPECIFIC CHARACTERS OF BRITISH LIZARDS	81
XI.	THE FRAGILITY OF THE TAIL IN LIZARDS	102
XII.	COLOUR VARIATION IN LIZARDS	115
XIII.	THE LIMBS OF LIZARDS	128

PART II

	COUNTY AND VICE-COUNTY DIVISIONS OF THE BRITISH ISLES	145
XIV.	COUNTY AND LOCAL DISTRIBUTION	149
XV.	PENINSULA PROVINCE. CHANNEL PROVINCE	158
XVI.	THAMES PROVINCE. OUSE PROVINCE. SEVERN PROVINCE	169

CONTENTS

CHAP.		PAGE
XVII.	SOUTH WALES, NORTH WALES, TRENT, MERSEY, HUMBER, TYNE, AND LAKES PROVINCES	176
XVIII.	SCOTLAND	186
XIX.	IRELAND	193
XX.	SUMMARY OF LOCAL DISTRIBUTION	195
	APPENDIX	205
	INDEX	209

ILLUSTRATIONS

SLOW-WORM		*Frontispiece*
1. SLOW-WORM		*To face p.* 28
2. SLOW-WORM		,, 30
3. BLUNT-TAILED SLOW-WORM		,, 32
4. FEMALE SLOW-WORM WITH YOUNG ONES		,, 38
5. FEMALE COMMON LIZARD		,, 46
6. MALE AND FEMALE COMMON LIZARDS		,, 49
7. COMMON LIZARD (GRAVID FEMALE)		,, 52
8. MALE AND FEMALE SAND LIZARDS		,, 56
9. SAND LIZARD (MALE)		,, 60
10. SAND LIZARD (GRAVID FEMALE)		,, 62
11. GREEN LIZARD		,, 72
12. GREEN LIZARD (VENTRAL SURFACE)		,, 74
13. WALL LIZARD		,, 76
14. WALL LIZARD (MALE)		,, 77
15. ATTITUDES OF WALL LIZARDS		,, 78
16. WALL LIZARD SHOWING FIGHT		,, 80
17. TYPICAL LIZARD'S HEAD (DORSAL ASPECT)		,, 86
18. TYPICAL LIZARD'S HEAD (LATERAL ASPECT)		,, 88
19. TYPICAL LIZARD'S HEAD (VENTRAL ASPECT)		,, 89
20. HEAD OF INDIAN SLOW-WORM (SCALING)		,, 90
21. HEAD SCALES OF COMMON LIZARD		,, 92
22. HEAD SCALES OF SAND LIZARD		,, 93
23. LATERAL ASPECT OF SAND LIZARD		,, 94
24. VENTRAL SCALING OF GREEN LIZARD		,, 95

ILLUSTRATIONS

25. HEAD OF GREEN LIZARD (DORSAL ASPECT) . . *To face p.* 97
26. WALL LIZARD . . . . . ,, 98
27. TAIL OF SLOW-WORM IN PROCESS OF FRACTURE . ,, 106
28. DISSECTIONS OF FRACTURED TAIL IN LIZARDS . ,, 108

DIAGRAMS.

FIG. 1. ARRANGEMENT OF TAIL MUSCLES . . . 110
,, 2. RELATION OF CAUDAL SCALES TO FRACTURE . . 111
,, 3. SECTION OF TAIL 112

BRITISH LIZARDS

CHAPTER I

INTRODUCTORY

HOW TO DESCRIBE AN ANIMAL — DISTRIBUTION — MORPHOLOGY — PHYSIOLOGY — REPRODUCTION — EMBRYOLOGY — PALÆONTOLOGY — SPECIFIC CHARACTERS—EVOLUTION.

BEFORE entering upon the detailed account of the lizards found in the British Isles it will be well to indicate what would be necessary in order to give a complete picture of these reptiles. That is to say, we should have a very clear idea of what is involved in the full description of any animal, because such a description does not come within the province of the field naturalist for whom this book is specially intended. There are but few people who realise how many various aspects of animal life must be taken into consideration in order to see that life as a whole.

Most of us who study animals at all confine our attention to one or two of those aspects to the neglect of others. This is indeed a necessity in these days of specialisation, when we have realised that it is more than the work of a lifetime for any one man to thoroughly work out the life-history of a single species from every point of view. But it is important that the field naturalist should accurately appreciate the particular aspects which are open to his investigation, and it is no less important that he should realise the existence of other points of view, the investigation of which must fall to the lot of others. That does not imply that his *knowledge* of an animal must be limited to those aspects which he himself can inquire into, but it does imply the recognition of the fact that there are other aspects of animals than those which can be observed out of doors. Therefore we say that the very first thing the field naturalist should know about the animal kingdom is what the description of an animal involves. That is by no means such a simple matter as might appear. It may be explained by an illustration. Suppose for a moment that the observer discovers an animal which, as far as he is able to ascertain, is something which has not been described before, a new species. He is anxious to draw up a description of it to present to a meeting of some society, so that his hearers may get a complete idea of his discovery. He will probably find that the task of fully describing one animal is quite beyond his powers, and he would find this out as he went on. He would begin, perhaps, by stating the locality in which he found the specimen, the only locality in which it was at the time known to occur. This statement is the *Geographical Distribution* or *Zoogeography* of the animal, and is one aspect of animal description. It is, in other words, its distribution *in Space* as far as is known. He would then probably proceed to describe the general form and appearance of the animal—its shape, colour, possession of limbs, wings, fins, and other obvious external structures, or the absence of these. If minute in size, he would examine it under the microscope; if large, he would examine its internal structure by dissection. This is a second aspect of the animal, that of its *structure* or *Morphology*. This includes both naked-eye and microscopic structures. By this study he would determine on what plan the animal is built up, and as the result of the knowledge thus gained he would be able to say whether the animal was a bird, fish, insect, and so on. This is the aspect of animals which is most studied in zoological laboratories, but which the field naturalist usually does not spend much time over. He is much more interested in recording and observing how the animal lives its life, and adapts itself to its surroundings. The *functions* performed by all the structures of the body interest him more than the method on which those structures are built up. In describing his discovery from this third point of view he is describing the *Physiology* of the animal, or the manner in which the functions are performed during life. This is, again, an immense subject, and he will soon find that he is quite unable to account for all that he sees. But he will also perceive that all the functions which the animal is capable of performing are one of three kinds. They are either concerned with (*a*) *Nutrition*, (*b*) *Reproduction*, or if neither of these, they are (*c*) directed to *bringing the animal into Relation with the world around* it. Every function is one of these three kinds. Breathing by gills, lungs, or the surface of the body is a matter of keeping the body nourished; so are the various methods adopted by animals to excrete waste products; so is the circulation of blood; so is digestion,—all are functions of Nutrition.

The special means adopted to reproduce offspring constitute the *Reproductive functions*, whether these be simply growing buds, or more complicated methods. Everything that is not either a nutritive or a reproductive function belongs to the third group of functions, those by which the animal comes into contact with its surroundings. Sight, hearing, touch, smell, taste, consciousness, memory, thought, ideation, and so forth, are *all functions of Relation*. One cannot conceive of any physiological function which is not directed to one of these three ends. So that our naturalist has now described his animal from three distinct aspects, and, although that has involved much labour, it by no means exhausts the matter. A further investigation may lead him to find out that his new discovery, though now so rare, was at one period of the world's history a much more common animal. There may be many *fossil* examples of a similar creature. He must therefore describe its distribution *in Time,* or its *Palæontology,* as well as its distribution in present space. The past and present distribution of the same forms of life present some most interesting problems, and the two do not by any means necessarily coincide. Thus he has completed a fourth aspect. But then there is another. What is it that makes this animal different from all others, and justifies its being regarded as a new form to science? What characters has it which are peculiar to itself? Some of its structures are common to many animals, but some there are which no other animal possesses, and on account of these the discovery is recognised as a new species. This is the aspect of *Specific characters.* Then there is an aspect which is really a combination of the morphological and the physiological, but which is such a large subject that it is regarded as a separate aspect—namely, the study of the various changes in form and function through which an organism passes before it reaches the stage of maturity. This is the *embryological aspect,* or the study of *Embryology.* Lastly, there is the *philosophical* aspect of animal life, that which studies the connection of one kind of animal with another, their relationships, their origin, their future, their association. This is the aspect of *Evolution*, which includes the study of the most fascinating portion of biology, and is largely a theoretical study as well as a practical one. It does not refer to an *individual*, but to a group of individuals. We do not speak of the evolution of *a horse*, but that of *the horse* regarded as a species of animal.

Thus we see that there are more aspects of an animal that must be taken up in order to get a complete description of it than we might suppose at first sight. It is practically impossible for any one man to make himself familiar with all that is known of all these aspects even for a very few animals. Each aspect is a study so far-reaching in itself that *one* is more than most of us can manage to learn thoroughly. But it is of the greatest importance to remember that in describing an animal all these points of view must be considered before a complete description has been given.

For outdoor work the *Physiological*, the *Geographical*, and the *Specific characters* are the most important aspects. Structure must not be lost sight of, for on that alone do naturalists classify animals, but it is studied here more in its relation to function than for its own sake. The main questions the field naturalist has to study are:—What animals live in a given region? What characters make them the species they are? How are they related to other living or extinct forms? How do they live their life?

INTRODUCTORY

If my readers have appreciated the foregoing remarks, it will be quite evident that some aspects of animal life are adapted for the field naturalist's method of work, and can, indeed, be done by no one else, whilst other aspects have to be studied in the laboratory. There is no question of the relative value of these methods, it is simply that they are distinct aspects, and it seldom happens that the same individual is able to devote himself to both lines of investigation. But the object of a book should be to give the field worker just sufficient information from those points of view which he himself does *not* work which will enable him more thoroughly to understand the phenomena which come under his observation out of doors. Therefore we shall first of all discuss very simply and briefly the place of British lizards in the animal kingdom, their structure, and methods of reproduction, and then conclude our sketch of the subject with the description of those aspects of the life of these creatures which are open to every field naturalist to see for himself.

CHAPTER II

THE ORDER LACERTILIA

DEFINITION OF LIZARD—CLASSIFICATION—GENERAL FACTS.

ALTHOUGH one can arrive at a definition of an order of animals only after minute consideration of their structure and relationships, it will be simpler for our present purpose to define what we mean by a lizard at once, and then see how that definition is arrived at.

Definition.—Lizards are Saurians which have the right and left halves of the lower jaws connected by a bony suture.

Such a definition indicates at once that structural characters alone are to be relied upon for classification. It also indicates that we cannot understand the definition of any one order of animals unless we also understand the definitions of other groups. In this particular case it becomes necessary to know what Saurians are before we understand what is meant by a lizard. It will be sufficient, perhaps, for our present purpose if we state that the Sauria are the most recently developed reptiles, and include both the Ophidia or Serpents and the Lacertilia or Lizards. Looking now at the definition above it becomes apparent that lizards are distinguished from serpents by the fact that in the former the two halves of the lower jaw are firmly united together by a bony suture or joint which allows of no distension. In the serpents, on the other hand, these two halves of the lower jaw are connected by an elastic ligament which allows of immense distension, an anatomical difference which we shall find has its functional counterpart in the different kinds of food swallowed. It is only necessary, further, to have a clear idea of what constitutes a Reptile. Briefly, Reptiles may be described as the only vertebrate animals which are cold-blooded, which breathe by lungs throughout life, and which have the skull joined on to the vertebral column by a single median condyle or articulating surface. These few characters mark them off distinctly from the other vertebrate animals — the Amphibians, the Fishes, the Birds, and the Mammals. So that the definition of a lizard, which at first sight, perhaps, seemed somewhat formidable, is easily reduced to simple everyday language. The important thing, of course, is to clearly distinguish between a lizard and any other reptile which is not a lizard—a snake for instance; and when we consider how very like a snake the common slow-worm appears, it is at once evident that accurate classification must be founded upon a basis of structure.

It is no part of this work to enter upon the structural characters of all the orders of Reptiles; it will be sufficient now if we indicate in tabular form what those orders are (as far as living reptiles are concerned, and omitting the extinct forms), when the position of the lizards will be more clearly apparent.

Class Reptilia.
- Order Chelonia (turtles and tortoises).
- Order Crocodilia (crocodiles, etc.).
- Order Squamata or Sauria.
  - Suborder Ophidia (serpents).
  - Suborder Lacertilia (lizards).

We see, then, from the above classification that we have to deal with one suborder of the class of Reptiles, namely, the Lacertilia. We have already defined this group, and seen how the definition is arrived at. The next thing is to look at the group *as a whole*, which will enable us to appreciate the position which is occupied by the British members of it.

The Lacertilia or Lizards.—Included in this great suborder of lizards there are some 1800 species, only five of which come into the limits of this book. Four of these are found to belong to the family Lacertidæ, the remaining one, the slow-worm, to the family Anguidæ. With the other numerous families of lizards we have at present nothing to do, as we can obtain all the information required for our purpose from these two families.

Most lizards are found on examination to possess two pairs of limbs, an anterior pair and a posterior pair, all these limbs being built up on the typical vertebral type, such as is commonly studied in the frog, and known as the pentadactyloid type. Some species, however, show no indication of any external limbs at all, giving them a snake-like appearance to the eye, an example of which is to be seen in the slow-worm. The great majority have eyelids, which are movable, a feature which distinguishes these members from snakes which have no movable eyelids. The external covering in most is in the form of scales. The great interest of the group is their immense variation. "They exhibit a great, almost endless, variety in shape, size, and structure, in adaptation to their surroundings. Most of these modifications are restricted to the external organs, or rather to those which come into direct contact with the outer world, namely, the skin, the limbs, the tail, or the tongue. The majority are terrestrial, but there are also semi-aquatic forms. There are climbing, swiftly running, and even flying forms, whilst others lead a subterranean life like earthworms. Most of them live on animal food, varying from tiny insects and worms to birds and mammals, while others live on vegetable diet. According to this diet, the teeth and the whole digestive tract are modified. The intestine is relatively short in the carnivorous, long in the herbivorous species. But swiftness, the apparatus necessary for climbing, running, and digging, the mechanism of the tongue, the armament and muscles of the jaws, stand also in correlation with the kind of food and with the way in which it has to be procured."[1]

In colouring the lizards present again immense variation, according to their habitat. Those which are dwellers in deserts approximate to the colour of the sandy surroundings, being brownish or yellowish red. Many which live amongst luxurious vegetation are brilliantly coloured, and a large number have the power of more or less changing their hue, a characteristic particularly associated with the Chameleon family. A curious property of many lizards is the readiness with which a portion of the tail breaks off, and the capacity for reproducing more or less perfectly the lost portion, the regenerated part · differing, however, in some details from the original tail. Like the snakes, lizards cast their slough periodically, sometimes whole, sometimes in pieces. Taking the Lacertilia as a whole, the majority reproduce their young by depositing eggs, that is, they are oviparous, the "shell" being either hard (as in the green lizard and the sand lizard) or more membraneous. These latter eggs increase in size after being deposited, from the taking in of moisture. Other species lay their

[1] Dr. Gadow, *Amphibia and Reptiles*, p. 492.

eggs just as the embryos are at full time, that is, they are ovo-viviparous; while still others bring forth their young alive, that is, are viviparous.

As regards their distribution the Lacertilia are almost universally found, or at least some of them. The Lacertidæ, to which most of the British species belong, are confined to the old world, but are absent from Madagascar. The Anguidæ, the family of the slow-worm, occur "in North and South America, in Europe and the Mediterranean parts of North Africa, and in Trans-Gangetic India." The detailed distribution of the several British species will be referred to later.

With this brief description we must leave the Lacertilia as a whole, and consider the structure of one of them in some detail.

CHAPTER III

THE ANATOMY OF THE LIZARDS

THE SKELETON, EXO-SKELETON AND ENDO-SKELETON—NOSTRILS—EYES—AUDITORY APERTURE—CLOACAL APERTURE—ALIMENTARY TRACT—LIVER—HEART—PANCREAS—SPLEEN—TESTES—OVARIES—BLADDER—BRAIN.

IN this chapter it is intended to give a short description of the more prominent anatomical characters of a lizard, so that the field naturalist may be able to understand any dissections which he may have access to in museums, and may be able to recognise the various parts in a dissection which he may do for himself. We select the green lizard for subject of description, because it is larger than the other British species, and also because those who wish to study the structure for themselves can always obtain this species from dealers in animals at a small cost. Moreover, since four of the five species we have to consider belong to this same family, it is obviously more useful to take this as our type, leaving the anatomical pecul-

THE ANATOMY OF THE LIZARDS

iarities of the slow-worm to be mentioned separately. More minute details of structure would be beyond the province of this work, and the student is referred for these to the text-books of zoology.

Skeleton.—The exo-skeleton, or body-covering, consists of scales which overlap each other. (The specific arrangement of head scales will be dealt with later.) The scales are derived from the epidermis. They vary in size, character, and arrangement in different parts of the body: those on the dorsal aspect of the body being small and hexagonal and slightly keeled; those on the ventral or belly surface are much larger and arranged in longitudinal series; whilst those on the tail are of the same nature all round the circumference, and are longer than broad, keeled and arranged in transverse series. This causes the annulated appearance of the tail.

Where the neck joins the trunk there is a fold of skin, in front of which the neck scales are larger than those more anterior still. The head scales are large. The anterior margin of the anal orifice or cloacal opening is formed by a large scale or plate, the pre-anal plate. A little careful study of these points in a lizard will enable the field naturalist to determine the part of the body to which a portion of a slough belongs, and if that slough is from the body or head the species may also be known.

The endo-skeleton, or bony-skeleton, may be prepared for examination by allowing the bones which have been partially stripped of muscles, to soak in water for some time. The soft parts which are left will soon decay, and can then readily be stripped off, leaving the bones clean. A quicker method is to boil the specimen for a quarter of an hour, which renders the soft parts easily detachable.

Having, in one or other way, prepared a clean skeleton, observe first the vertebral column. Eight vertebræ are found in the cervical or neck region, then follow twenty-two in the trunk region; behind these, two vertebræ in the sacral region to which the pelvis is joined; and, lastly, a number of vertebræ in the tail, the number of which vary in different specimens.

The ribs arise in pairs from the vertebræ, but not from all. They are largest in the front part of the chest, where they are joined to the sternum or breastbone, smaller in front of this, and become gradually smaller as we trace them backwards from the chest to the sacral region.

Note particularly the shape of the large vertebræ. They are concave in front, convex behind, the type of vertebræ called procœlous. They thus form a series of cup-and-ball joints, which are admirably adapted for flexibility and general ease of motion. Five ribs will be found to articulate with the sternum, the hinder ribs of the thorax do not reach it. In the neck region ribs will be found arising from the last

THE ANATOMY OF THE LIZARDS

five vertebræ, in this case also not being attached to the sternum.

A single protuberance from the occipital bone, the condyle, joins the skull to the first cervical vertebra or atlas.

The bones of the fore-limb are those usually found in vertebrate limbs, namely, humerus, radius (smaller than the) ulna, carpal or wrist bones, and five clawed fingers or digits.

Similarly, in the hind limb are found, the femur or thigh bone, tibia (larger than the) fibula, tarsal or ankle bones, and five toes or digits.

An external examination of a lizard shows that the animal may be divided into—a head, which is somewhat flat; a neck, separated from the trunk by a slightly narrowed part; the trunk, ending abruptly at the tail, which is round and gradually tapers to a fine point. The tail, if it be intact, is longer than all the rest of the lizard. The sides of the trunk are not convex, but rather flattened, and from their lower borders the fore and hind limbs spring. On both hand and foot the first digit is the shortest; on the hand the second and third digits are the longest; on the foot the fourth is the longest.

The openings on the external surface are eight in number. They consist of the large wide mouth; the two anterior nostrils, one on each side of the front of the snout; the two eyes, about half-way between the nostrils and the auditory opening; the auditory aperture just behind the posterior angle of the mouth (with the delicate tympanic membrane covering); and, lastly, the anal or cloacal opening at the root of the tail—a transverse slit.

Coming now to the internal structure of the lizard, we note first the alimentary tract. On the floor of the mouth is the long narrow tongue, bifid in front, but not so deeply divided as in a snake. The teeth are small and conical, and there are, of course, no fangs. The gullet or œsophagus leads to the stomach, which lies under the liver. The stomach is a strong muscular tube which is continued as the small intestine, this in its turn ending in the large intestine and rectum. The rectum is of greater dimensions transversely, and gives off a small pouch, the cæcum.

The liver is a large brown organ in the middle of the body with a duct to the gall-bladder, the latter being usually recognisable by its green colour from the bile within it. The pancreas is a narrow whitish structure between the stomach and intestine, and the small reddish spleen is near the posterior end of the stomach. In the male, the two oval white testes will be seen, the right one being placed farther forwards than the left. In the female, the two ovaries are situated rather more posteriorly than the testes in the male, and show rounded elevations, due to the eggs within. The urinary bladder is a thin sac. There are two kidneys, dark brown in colour, each consisting of two lobes. The ducts from these urino-genital organs open into the cloaca.

The three-chambered heart consists of a single ventricle and two auricles, right and left. Three main arteries come from the base of the ventricle, namely, the pulmonary artery carrying blood to the lungs, and the right and left aortæ. These two vessels after arching to either side, bend round the gullet, and unite to form one vessel, the dorsal aorta, which distributes the blood, by means of its branches, to the posterior part of the body. The great veins which bring the blood to the heart, empty into a venous sinus, or directly into the right auricle.

The respiratory system consists of a windpipe or trachea, which divides into two bronchi, and each of these communicates with the corresponding lung. Each lung is a very thin sac, the posterior part being the thinner, the walls of which are made up of a network of ridges, which support the vessels through which the exchange of oxygen and impure products takes place.

If the brain be exposed by removing the roof of the skull, we note from before backwards the olfactory lobes, cerebral hemispheres, the pineal body, optic lobes, small cerebellum, and the medulla oblongata, this last being continuous with the spinal cord. Various cranial nerves will be seen emerging.

The foregoing are the principal points which the field naturalist will be concerned with. Those who wish to examine in greater detail the anatomy of a lizard are recommended to study the description given in Professor T. J. Parker's practical book on *Zootomy*, on which the above brief sketch is based.

The anatomical arrangements in lizards which are of most interest to field naturalists, and which come within the scope of this work, are those in connection with the process of feeding. The reason for this, of course, is that the lizards offer a striking comparison and contrast with the snakes in the matter of dealing with their prey, and in the structural adaptations of the jaws and skull for mastication. The subject has recently been worked out by Dr. Charnock Bradley (Professor of Anatomy in the Royal Veterinary College, Edinburgh); and his paper, which is in course of publication in the *Zoologische Jahrbücher*,[1] is one which all students of reptilian morphology should read. Dr. Bradley has been kind enough to send me the manuscript of his paper, from which what follows on this subject is quoted. The paper is "an endeavour to throw some light on the peculiarities of the jaw movements of lizards. . . . On account of the conveniently large size, *Varanus bivittatus* was examined in the first instance, and it was found that this animal formed a very excellent type with which to compare the muscles of the smaller lizards. In addition to Varanus, *Lacerta agilis* and *viridis* . . . have also been examined. The process of mastication was

[1] "The Muscles of Mastication and the Movements of the Skull, Lacertilia," vol. xviii. p. 475.

watched in the living *L. agilis* and *viridis*, and in these animals also the fresh skull was examined in order to discover the possibilities of movement between the various parts."

It was long ago pointed out that the movements of the jaws in lizards did not consist merely in the depression and elevation of the lower jaw, but that there was along with this a corresponding elevation and depression of the upper jaw. This movement of the upper jaw was supposed to take place along two lines—first, between the frontal and parietal bones; and second, between the parietal bones and the occipital. Dr. Bradley comes to a different conclusion. "It may be stated at once that the anterior line of movement, as described by Nitzsch, does not exist. The joint between the frontal and parietal bones is not movable. Certainly, in the skull of a lizard, such as *L. viridis*, a certain bending can be produced, but it is dependent upon the thinness of the bones, and not upon any peculiarity in the line of fusion of frontal and parietal bones. In the larger lizards, and in those with thicker cranial bones, such a bending is not possible unless extreme force is used." . . . "The two halves of the mandible are very loosely joined together at the symphysis. It appears not unreasonable to expect that in the living animal there is some degree of rotation of each half of the mandible about its own long axis. Such rotation, at any rate, can be very readily produced in a fresh skull."

After describing in detail the movements of the different segments of the skull, Dr. Bradley sums up the effect of these movements thus: "Least movement occurs in the neighbourhood of the ends of the projecting lateral occipitals, in which region, it may be remarked, are the upper ends of the quadrate bones. There is elevation of the frontal segment at the same time as the mandible is depressed, and at the same time there is a narrowing of the mouth, which narrowing is greatest posteriorly. When the mouth is closed, the parts are restored to the condition of rest, *i.e.* there is depression of the frontal segment, and abduction of the pterygo-palatine arch, lower end of the quadrate and posterior part of the mandible. This results in an increase in the transverse diameter of the mouth, the increase being greatest posteriorly. If the frontal segment be more forcibly depressed, the basipterygoid processes of the sphenoid exert their wedge-like action upon the pterygoid, so producing further abduction. Therefore, when the frontal segment is depressed, the transverse diameter of the mouth is increased.

"The advantage of the abduction and adduction of the jaws is obvious when we remember the nature and condition of the food of lizards. Their prey is always living, and therefore we may presume desirous of escape. Supposing the victim to be a worm, the following is apparently the manner in which the lizard succeeds in swallowing it. From its conformation the

THE ANATOMY OF THE LIZARDS

worm must be seized by one end. This having been done, in order that deglutition may be accomplished, the lizard must again open its mouth to the end that a further hold may be obtained upon the elongated prey. The mouth being open, were there no provision to prevent it, the squirming worm might regain its freedom. This accident, however, is prevented by the adduction of the previously abducted jaws, which firmly grip that portion of the worm which is contained in the mouth. This process is repeated until the whole of the worm has passed into the œsophagus. The grip by the pterygoid bones is rendered more secure by the pterygoidean teeth when such structures are present."

Dr. Bradley's most instructive paper is illustrated by a series of original drawings of the muscles and articulations concerned in the movements discussed.

Apart from the jaws, the lizards—or some of them —exhibit some striking anatomical contrasts among each other in the matter of limbs, and in the function of locomotion. This subject is dealt with later in a separate chapter in connection with the limbless slow-worm.

CHAPTER IV

THE SLOW-WORM, *ANGUIS FRAGILIS*

INTRODUCTORY — DISTRIBUTION — HAUNTS — HABITS — COLOUR — FOOD — REPRODUCTION — SPECIFIC CHARACTERS.

HAVING taken a brief survey of the lizards as a whole, and of the structure of a typical lizard, we are in a position to consider in detail the several British species. It is doubtless true that to many people lizards are only one degree less repulsive than snakes, in spite of the fact that lizards are absolutely innocuous reptiles. But it is equally certain that they have an ever-increasing number of friends, who have found out what delightful and interesting pets they are in vivaria. It is a sad reflection, however,—notwithstanding the vast increase in the number of books on natural history, and therefore, presumably, in the spread of knowledge about animals;—that they are still remorselessly slaughtered by the majority of those who encounter them. More particularly is this the case of the slow-worm or blind-worm, concerning which species an astonishing amount of ignorance still prevails. The fact that this unfortunate lizard is devoid of external limbs is quite sufficient to assure its being regarded as a "poisonous snake" in the minds of rustics and others, and accordingly it is pitilessly persecuted wherever it is at all common. Happily it is so protectively coloured as to frequently escape observation, and its habit of lying perfectly still—hence the term slow-worm—also assists it to elude notice. Were it not that nature thus comes to the rescue, this and other species of perfectly harmless and beautiful reptiles would soon become extinct. Whatever excuse there may be for this mental attitude in the uneducated classes, there is certainly none for its prevalence amongst those who regard themselves as lovers of animals; and yet it is astonishing how some people can detest lizards, who are fond of many other species of animals. I know a naturalist who handles wasps and other creatures which sometimes behave in anything but a friendly way, but who would not handle a slow-worm under any consideration whatever. Even field naturalists, or perhaps one should say, members of field clubs, occasionally exhibit extraordinary lack of knowledge about the slow-worm; in proof of which I may mention that on no less than ten occasions since 1899 I have had reports of the occurrence of the rare British snake, the smooth snake (*Coronella austriaca*), every one of which turned out upon investigation to be nothing more nor less than so many captures of slow-worms! I do not mean to insinuate that such ignorance is common amongst those who work at outdoor natural history, but one is driven to the conclusion that there is room for improvement. Such a mistake as this makes it necessary to point out the distinction between a limbless lizard like the slow-worm, and a snake of any species. It may be admitted at once that the general form of this lizard is snakelike, that is, it is possessed of a long, slender body without any obvious indications of limbs, and no very marked separation of the tail from the body. The same remark practically applies to an eel, which means, of course, that such a superficial description of a creature is of no value whatever as a means of classification. Three simple structural points, all of which can be seen without any dissection, are amply sufficient to identify the slow-worm as a lizard, and to separate it from the snakes, at any rate as far as British reptiles are concerned, which is all we need consider here. First of all, the most casual observer could hardly fail to notice that the slow-worm has *eyelids*; the snakes have no eyelids. How this creature came by its other popular name of blind-worm, considering the brilliancy of its eyes, is difficult to understand, unless it was from seeing it with the eyes closed during hibernation. Secondly, if the belly scales be examined, it will be seen that they are made up of a number of rows in the slow-worm (as in other lizards); while in the snakes a single large broad scale extends from one side of the belly to the other. Thirdly, the tail in the slow-worm is as long as the body; in the snakes it is shorter than the body. On dissection, other differences would become apparent, and it may be convenient here to sum these distinctions up in tabular form for reference.

Lacertilia or Lizards.	Ophidia or Snakes.
Limbs present or rudiments.	Limbs absent.
Eyelids present.	Eyelids absent.
Belly scales in several rows.	Belly scales in one row.
Jaws firmly united.	Jaws widely distensible.
Teeth conical (as a rule).	Teeth recurved.
Tongue notched.	Tongue deeply bifid.
All are innocuous.	One British species venomous.
Sternum present.	Sternum absent.
Urinary bladder present.	Urinary bladder absent.

It is the rudimentary limbs that have caused the blind-worm to be regarded as a snake by the ignorant. No sign of these appears externally, but a careful dissection reveals the presence of the rudimentary pelvic girdle which, in the limbed forms, articulates with the hind limbs. This lizard is from this point of view, therefore, intermediate between the snakes and lizards with limbs,—one of the many connecting links found in nature indicating the gradual evolution of creatures from generalised to specialised types.

Distribution.—The slow-worm, or blind-worm, is

found, in more or less abundance, universally in Europe, with the exception of the extreme northern portions of the Continent, where the cold is too severe for reptile life to flourish. In the British Isles it is common—in England, Scotland, and Wales, but does not occur in Ireland. It seems to occur in all the counties, but is much more numerous in some localities than in others. In my own experience I have found it more abundantly in the south-western counties of England than in the eastern or northern counties, and in Wales it is found in great numbers in the southern parts. I have been much struck with its rarity in some counties, where the snakes were common, and where the viviparous common lizard was plentiful. Such a case is found in the Broadland district of Norfolk, where one may capture a dozen adders in a day and never see a slow-worm in the same time. In Dorset, on the other hand, where both adders and ring-snakes are common, the slow-worm is also plentiful. Most counties, however, contain some suitable spots where search will be rewarded.

Description.—The general appearance of this lizard is too familiar to need detailed description, and a glance at the illustrations in this book will give an excellent idea of its postures and attitudes. Great variety is seen in size and colour. As the result of a large series of measurements of specimens taken from different parts of the country, we may state the average size of a full-grown specimen to be between

SLOW-WORM.

[Facing p. 28.

THE SLOW-WORM, ANGUIS FRAGILIS

12 and 15 inches. In making such a measurement the observer should carefully examine the tail, to be certain it is all there. Very many specimens have lost a portion of the tail, and this can be recognised by the unusually blunt ending of the organ in those cases. If the tail measures less than half the total length, it has almost certainly been mutilated at some time or other. In the females about half the total length is tail, in males rather more than half the total length, which reminds us that in snakes also the tail is longer in males than in females. The spot where the tail begins can be readily recognised by noting the large anal scale, which is the most posterior scale on the ventral aspect of the belly.

There is no lateral fold in this lizard, nor any fold in the neck region, and, as we have said, no indication at all of external limbs. The whole creature is covered with very smooth shining scales, which are rounded, not hexagonal. Those on the head are larger than those elsewhere. In this species the teeth "are curved backwards, fang-shaped, and have a faint longitudinal groove on their anterior surface."[1] The position of the ear is difficult to determine, as it has the opening partially hidden from view by the scales in that region. The eyes are small but very bright and noticeable, in spite of the popular misnomer of blind-worm. A marked characteristic is the great smoothness of the skin; in fact, it would be hard to

[1] Gadow, *Amphibia and Reptiles*, p. 539.

mention any animal which is so smooth to the touch, and which is at the same time free from any suspicion of slime. The skin is, of course, quite dry. Its metallic lustre is well known, giving the appearance of polished copper or silver, according to the colour variation. A few moments of watching will show the observer the movable eyelids and the protrusible notched tongue, black in colour. The motion of the tongue is much more deliberate than in the case of the snakes, not a rapid quivering, but a somewhat slow protrusion and withdrawal. After swallowing a slug it is amusing to see the slow-worm lick its jaws for a minute or two with the tongue, at the same time usually giving some huge yawns and gapes.

As regards the size that the slow-worm attains, very various statements have been made. It is not at all uncommon to find a specimen 15 or 16 inches long, and I once captured a beautiful bright copper-coloured male in a wood in Dorset which measured $17\frac{1}{2}$ inches. This is the largest that I have personally taken, but they have been reported up to 18 inches. The specimen just mentioned did not grow any longer during the next year and a half that he inhabited my vivarium.

There are no very prominent markings on this species, but a close inspection will reveal the existence of a thin, dark line along the side of the body, somewhat similar in appearance to the lateral line in fishes. A similar dark line may be seen running down the

SLOW-WORM.
(*Drops of dew on the body.*)

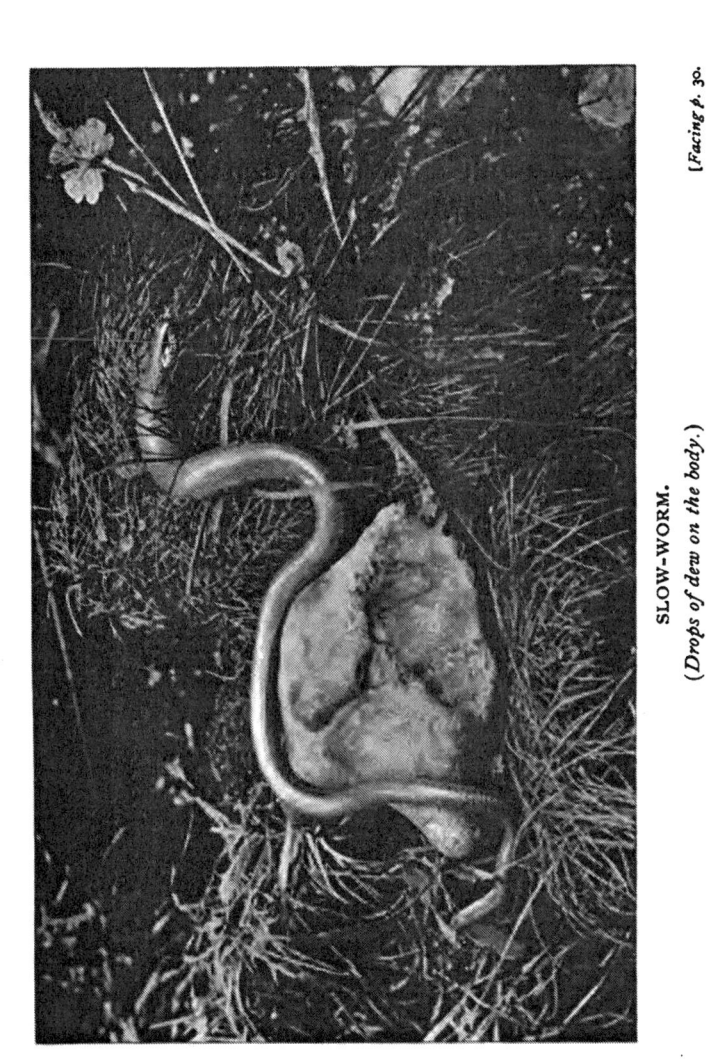

[*Facing p.* 30.

THE SLOW-WORM, *ANGUIS FRAGILIS*

middle line of the back. The lateral line is distinctly seen in the illustration.

Habits.—It is no easy task to gain a clear idea of the habits of lizards in nature, as they are not creatures which obtrude themselves upon the notice. Still, continuous searching for these reptiles will convince the naturalist that they live a simple and quiet life without much variety in it. He will come to this conclusion from finding the great majority of his specimens under very similar circumstances. If the temperature be cool, the slow-worm remains under the covering protection of vegetation or under stones, particularly flat tombstones in country churchyards. Hence, in obedience to that love of warmth and sunshine which is inherent in reptiles, they emerge to sun themselves on grassy banks on country roadsides or secluded footpaths. Lying perfectly still amongst the grass on such a bank, it is by no means easy to see the animal even when it is straight in front of the observer. If approached quietly, the slow-worm usually remains motionless; and I remember once standing within four feet of one sunning itself in this way and endeavouring to indicate its position to a companion who was with me, but in vain. He simply could not see it, although his eyes roamed over every blade of grass in the spot I described. Very carefully and slowly I brought my hand down on to the slow-worm, which made no attempt to move though watching me all the time, and not until I actually touched it could he make out the animal. I mention this because there is no doubt that it is the reason why these lizards are so seldom seen by some people who are not in the habit of observing them. Their protective colouring and habitual immobility render them difficult to find.

Once grasped in the hand there is grave danger of a catastrophe to the tail, unless care is taken to allow the creature to entwine itself amongst the fingers, which slow-worms are very fond of doing. If they are held up by the neck, firmly gripped by the thumb and finger as if they were something which might have to be dropped very suddenly—as many hold them,—they will probably lash themselves wildly from side to side and at the same time stiffen the muscles of the tail. It is an energetic protest against the method of handling. In such a case a part of the tail is very apt to be broken off, due to the great fragility possessed by this organ, hence the specific name *fragilis*. No danger of this accident need be apprehended if the captor will allow the slow-worm to rest on the whole of the palm of the hand and insert its coils between the fingers. The cause of this easy separation of a part of the tail has recently been investigated, and is dealt with in a subsequent chapter. It is a phenomenon seen in many species of lizards, and is of use to them in assisting evasion of their enemies. Other reptiles feed upon slow-worms, and if the pursuer catches the slow-worm by the tail, and the

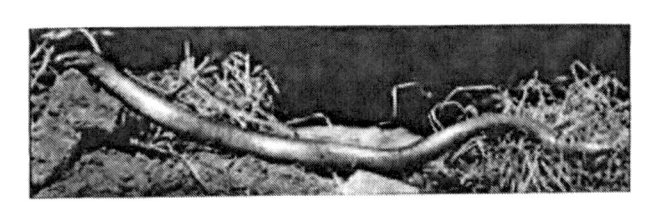

SLOW-WORM : BLUNT TAIL.

[*Facing p.* 32.

THE SLOW-WORM, *ANGUIS FRAGILIS*

slow-worm drops the terminal few inches, both parties attain their end. The slow-worm saves its life at the expense of a little tail, the enemy gets its food, and is probably also satisfied.

The movement of a slow-worm upon the ground is a wonderful thing to watch. It is almost uncanny,—this smooth, even, gliding amongst the grass without the slightest appearance of the putting forth of any effort. Very rapid it is, too, at times, though often slow and always quiet. The term slow-worm is probably due to the fact that the reptile is slow to move when observed. It cannot be accurately given to describe individual movements, many of which are extremely rapid. Very often, if the creature be encountered as it is moving along, it will stop and become motionless, a habit which may also have had its place in the origin of this term, and one which is too often the immediate cause of the cruel persecution meted out to it.

Colour Variation.—As in most reptiles, a great range of colour variation is found The different appearances are due mainly to the influence of the two factors of age and sex, the former having the most obvious influence. When first born the young slow-worms are silvery white above, with very black bellies, the dark line down the middle of the back being prominent. They are extremely attractive at this stage, very active and brilliant. As they grow older the colours change a good deal and vary much.

The black belly gives place to a mottled grey colour. The body may be grey or brownish, or the bright polished copper colour already mentioned. The old specimens will be found sometimes mottled with blue. No hard-and-fast rules can be laid down, as the individuals vary so much.

Food.—Despite the various diets ascribed to the slow-worm, I have no hesitation in saying that the favourite and staple food consists of slugs, the common small grey garden slug for choice. The fact that the lizard has a non-distensible jaw of course precludes its swallowing large articles of diet which a snake can manage. The very young slow-worms are said to begin with small spiders and delicate insects,[1] but it is very astonishing how soon they, too, tackle the slugs. Very few days after birth this may be seen. Then earth-worms are said to be commonly eaten. My own invariable experience has been that a slow-worm will never eat earth-worms if it can get slugs, but they will eat them if nothing else is available. It should always be remembered that the food of a reptile, or other animal in captivity, is what the owner chooses to give it, and it by no means follows that it corresponds to its natural diet. Of course it should do so, and no person should keep an animal in captivity unless it can be fed on a diet very nearly that in its wild state. Slow-worms will eat worms in captivity, and insects, and possibly many other invertebrate creatures, but the

[1] Gadow, *Amphibia and Reptiles*, p. 540.

THE SLOW-WORM, *ANGUIS FRAGILIS*

result of much watching of them in nature has been to convince me that their one aim in life as far as food is concerned is to find good fat slugs, not too large. The number of these that a slow-worm will eat during an hour or so about sunset, when they feed most, is simply astonishing. I can vouch for a meal which consisted of seventeen slugs, the slow-worm being a large male 16 inches long. But the usual number taken seems to be from four to ten. Doubtless they feed during the night also, but not during the heat of the sun. In other words, when the slugs emerge from beneath stones and débris, then comes the slow-worm also. It is thus quite evident that a few slow-worms in a garden would be the best friends the gardener could have, but he, poor, ignorant, prejudiced fool, never loses an opportunity of slaughtering every one he finds on the estate. Surely it is not too much to expect that every field naturalist who comes in contact with people who have to work on the land should take the trouble to point out the economic value of our reptiles, and thus both save interesting lives of harmless creatures and at the same time prevent the disturbing of the balance of nature.

Very interesting to watch is the slow-worm feeding. The whole process is carried out very methodically and deliberately, and with evident satisfaction. The slug is seldom taken except when moving, and, as far as I have seen, never when dead. The slow-worm either gradually approaches or allows the slug to approach until the latter is within reaching distance, then poises its head in a delicate curve over the body of the slug, and with a quick movement—the only sign of haste in the whole business—seizes the mollusc by the middle. There is then a momentary pause as if to make sure that the grip is satisfactory, during which the reptile remains motionless while the slug exudes frothy bubbles. A sudden wide gape of the jaws and mouth—as far as the fixed jaws allow of distension—and the slug disappears head-first down the throat of the slow-worm, as if it were the direction of least resistance. Then follows much gaping and licking of jaws on the part of the slow-worm, and should another slug come into range the process is immediately repeated. The slug never takes the slightest notice of the slow-worm until it is seized, indeed they will frequently crawl all over the creature which a few minutes later feeds upon them. I have found that the larger slugs are refused, and so also are the brightly coloured ones; probably the latter are flavoured in a manner disagreeable to the slow-worm.

Slow-worms should never be allowed to be short of water. They drink frequently, and some are very fond of lying in a shallow bath, while others do not seem to care about it. They will also take milk.

CHAPTER V

THE SLOW-WORM, *ANGUIS FRAGILIS*—*continued*

REPRODUCTION—SLOUGHING—HIBERNATION—ENEMIES.

Reproduction.—Reproduction in lizards takes place in one of two ways, either by the deposition of the eggs by the mother when the eggs are but imperfectly developed, or, secondly, by the bringing forth of the young fully developed and able to look after themselves from birth. Both methods are found in British species, that of the slow-worm being the latter method. That is to say that *Anguis fragilis* is ovo-viviparous or viviparous. The two terms are used synonymously, but the former is the more descriptive, since it denotes the additional fact that the young have been carried to full time within an egg-membrane. The same process obtains in the adder. The egg-membrane is a very delicate transparent structure easily ruptured by the embryo when fully developed. This generally happens in August or September, the exact time depending upon the nature of the season. In a warm early spring the young slow-worms see the light in

August; in a later and colder season their advent is delayed until September. The number of the offspring varies a good deal, rarely less than four or six, but often as many as a dozen. Their size at birth also varies, probably with the age and size of the parent. Most we have seen have been very slightly under 2 inches long, but that they may sometimes be much larger than this the following quotation from *The Field Naturalist's Quarterly* (August 1902) will show. The writer is Rev. S. Cornish Watkins, who has for many years observed slow-worms in nature and captivity. The illustration opposite is the litter in question along with the mother.

"On September 8, 1902, I captured two female slow-worms under a large stone in a disused quarry. They were evidently heavy with young. I placed them in a glass-covered box, with some damp moss, and kept them liberally supplied with slugs, their favourite diet. Each of them has since then brought forth a litter of young ones, the one on September 20th, the other on the 24th, and in each case the litter numbered twelve. This is the maximum number stated to occur. I measured the young ones on the day of their birth and found that they were $3\frac{1}{2}$ inches in length, a size considerably larger than that given in the article referred to.[1] From the time of birth they were extremely active, and commenced to feed upon good-

[1] *The Field Naturalist's Quarterly*, vol. i. p. 181.

Photo by S. Cornish Watkins.

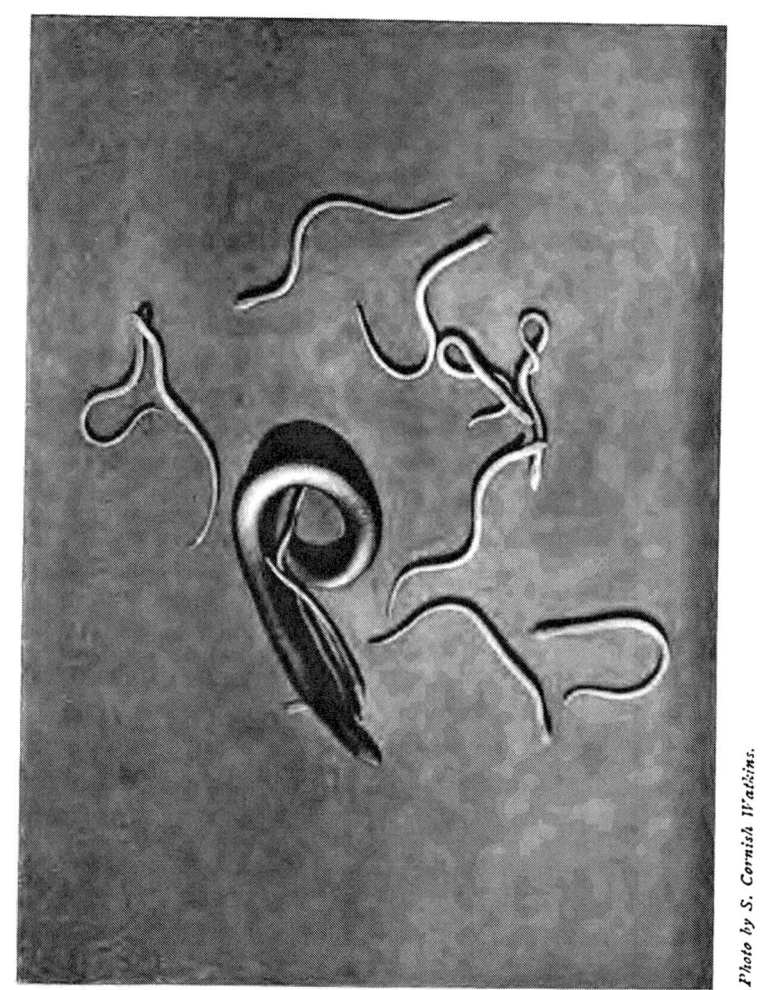

sized slugs the day after they were born. One of the young, on being handled, disgorged a slug quite half an inch in length which it had swallowed.

"I took several photographs of the mothers and the young together soon after birth, but on account of the extreme activity of the young ones they did not turn out as successful as I hoped. The most satisfactory perhaps is the one reproduced, but the incessant wriggling was most trying to the patience of the photographer."

This valuable note is of interest not only from the point of view of the size and number of young, but also as showing the short time which elapses before the young ones take to the favourite diet of their elders. The probability is that these were somewhat larger than the average young ones, and it is a fact that the slow-worms in Herefordshire, where this observation was made, are a large race. As a rule it is some six weeks before they attain the size of 3 inches. The following spring they will be found to be 5 or 6 inches long, and it takes four or five years for them to reach maturity.

Sloughing.—Like other reptiles of the lizard or snake groups, the slow-worm casts its slough periodically. I have described this process at length elsewhere,[1] and it will be sufficient here to state that the slough may be cast intact as one piece, or in several or many pieces. The slough is exceedingly delicate and therefore torn

[1] *British Serpents*, chap. vi.

with great ease, and can only be shed untorn if the slow-worm is able to glide through soft material during the process. Any sharp projecting point rubbing against the side of the creature will inevitably tear the slough before it is completely removed. The process starts at the jaws, and the lizard gradually crawls out of the slough, leaving it turned inside out as a rule, though the terminal portion of the tail slough may slip off unreversed. After sloughing, the slow-worm, like other reptiles, is more lively and feeds readily. The length of time between successive sloughings varies. Sloughing always happens after the slow-worm comes out of its winter quarters where it has been hibernating, and is generally repeated at intervals of six weeks or so during the months in the year when active life is in progress. The colouring of the reptile is more brilliant after sloughing than at other times. The slough is never eaten by lizards, as is the habit of some amphibians.

Hibernation.[1]—The slow-worm does not seem to feel the cold quite so much as some of our reptiles, and consequently may be found active later in the autumn than the snakes, and earlier in the spring. The exact date of commencing hibernation will depend upon the nature of the season, being earlier in a cold autumn, and later in a warm season. The month of October generally finds them in their winter quarters in most parts of the country, but in the extreme

[1] *British Serpents*, chap. vi.

south they are often seen later. The places selected for passing the period of torpidity are under thick masses of fallen autumn leaves, in burrows, and especially at the bottom of a heap of stones.

As far as I have observed, these lizards are not so apt to congregate in numbers to hibernate as do the snakes, but I have several times found six and seven together under masses of stone. Bright warm days in the winter months will sometimes bring them out of their hiding-place, especially in December, but they are rarely seen in January and early February, except in such counties as Cornwall and Dorset.

Enemies.—It is always of interest in sketching the life of any animal to note what are the other animals which prey upon it. In the case of our reptiles these enemies seem to be very few, for the simple reason that other reptiles are few in this country, and small reptiles have more to fear from larger reptiles than from most other animals. As far as the slow-worm is concerned, the adder or viper is by far the most dangerous and persistent foe, large numbers of slow-worms being taken by adders for food. Indeed, the adder is the only animal that the present writer is aware of which does this habitually, though it is quite possible that some large birds, rats, and the hedgehog, may also account for a certain number. An illustration elsewhere shows an adder which was captured in the act of swallowing a slow-worm, 4 inches of the tail of which were protruding from the mouth of the adder.[1] I captured this specimen under a large flat stone in an old disused quarry near the Monnow Valley in Herefordshire. It is now preserved in the Zoological Museum at Edinburgh University. Apart from the adder, man is the most persistent persecutor of the unfortunate slow-worm, and the fact that this harmless lizard does not shun the abodes of men as some reptiles do, tends to bring about its own destruction. Slow-worms are found more abundantly in the neighbourhood of villages and farms where there are gardens and walls and quarries than in bleak open moors, and it is therefore the more necessary that the utility and harmlessness of the creature should be widely recognised. Hedgerows they delight in, and a country lane near a village is more likely to reward the searcher than a lonely wood off the road. Unfortunately this very habit is their greatest danger.

Disposition.—As far as the character of the slow-worm is concerned it may challenge comparison with almost any animal, and is certainly more docile than most other reptiles. Though extremely timid at first, it rapidly becomes familiar with its owner, and will feed from the hand after a short time in the vivarium. But—and this is a point that many observers appear to have overlooked—slow-worms have their individual idiosyncrasies like other creatures, and some of them will exhibit a great tendency to bite. Even when they do, the small size of the teeth renders the bite

[1] *British Serpents*, p. 19.

THE SLOW-WORM, *ANGUIS FRAGILIS* 43

perfectly harmless, the only result being a series of small depressions on the skin showing the marks of the teeth. This exhibition of temper is generally seen in old females before the young are born, and I have had several such in my cages which would attempt to bite on every opportunity. The great majority, however, never attempt any such thing so long as they are handled carefully, being quiet and docile to a degree. They are extremely clean and take to life in a vivarium well, and therefore make most interesting pets. One cannot help being struck with their patience and curiosity. Time after time will they raise themselves up on to the tail to examine the side of the cage, until they may be said to stand on the tip of that organ, or very nearly so. Miss Hopley states that one of her slow-worms learned to recognise certain sounds made to attract her attention, and recognised a peculiar intonation of voice which was used to this specimen alone, even when at a distance of the far side of a room. In fact, the total sum of the characteristics of the slow-worm, or blind-worm, forms an entire negation of those implied by the popular names, since the creature is neither slow, blind, deaf, nor a worm.

This species will always be remembered by zoologists as that in which the discovery was made of the existence of a third or median eye in lizards. In the chapter on the anatomy of a lizard reference was made to the "pineal body," which comparative anatomists have demonstrated to be nothing more nor less than a degenerate eye. It is deeply embedded in the slow-worm, and is not at all affected by light; but in the remarkable New Zealand lizard, Sphenodon, this median eye is in a more perfect state of development. A detailed study of this pineal body would be beyond the province of this work, but its existence is a point of too great interest to be omitted altogether. Much has been written about it in zoological literature, which those who are specially interested can consult.

CHAPTER VI

THE COMMON LIZARD, *LACERTA VIVIPARA*

DISTRIBUTION—DESCRIPTION—HAUNTS—HABITS—FOOD —COLOUR VARIATION—REPRODUCTION.

Distribution. — The common lizard has a wide European distribution, characterised on the whole by a marked preference for high lands and mountainous districts, the low-lying areas being generally avoided, a feature which at the very outset provides one point of contrast with the sand lizard. Thus, *Lacerta vivipara* occurs in the mountains of Switzerland, and in all the following countries, namely, France, Germany, Italy, Belgium, Poland, and Russia. In the area to which this work particularly applies, the common lizard is to be noted as occurring in the four divisions of England, Scotland, Ireland, and Wales. Herein it differs from the slow-worm, which species, like the snakes, is absent from Ireland. It may be remarked in passing, that the statement so commonly made that there are no *reptiles* in Ireland is therefore inaccurate, the truth being that while there are no indigenous snakes in that country, lizards are not at all uncommon. Its local distribution in this country will be dealt with later, but I would just say here that, personally, I have not found this species in England to be markedly restricted to mountainous counties. Thus, while rather abundant in Norfolk, it is extremely rare in the hills of Monmouthshire; but the latter county is so rich in "cover" that the small lizards easily escape observation. It is peculiarly interesting from the distribution point of view, inasmuch as it is the only reptile to be found in Ireland, the sand lizard as well as the slow-worm having apparently come under the decree of banishment ascribed to St. Patrick. Why this species alone should have been permitted to set foot upon Irish soil is not quite clear, but very likely the viviparous lizard preceded the others in the spread of reptiles to the British Isles from the Continent at a time when the mainland was continuous from the Continent to Ireland. Ireland then became cut off from Great Britain, and Great Britain from the Continent, but in the case of Great Britain the viviparous lizard had been followed by the slow-worm and the sand lizard, as well as the three species of snakes before the separation occurred. Whether this is actually what took place or not, it is one view which gives a feasible explanation of the curious distribution of the British reptiles.

On the Continent this common or viviparous lizard is, as we have said, widely distributed, ranging " through

COMMON LIZARD (FEMALE).
LACERTA VIVIPARA.

Northern and Central Europe and Siberia to the Amoor country and the Island of Saghalien. It does not occur south of the Pyrenees or south of the Alps."[1] In Ireland its distribution seems to be irregular and somewhat local, "occurring, for instance, in the county of Meath, and in the south-eastern counties, *e.g.* Waterford."[1] A writer in *The Zoologist* (p. 7172) describes it as being unusually numerous in the year 1860 in the county of Down, where, he also states, the common lizard had never occurred before except in rare cases of single specimens.

Description.—A careful examination of the illustrations in this book, all of which are from photographs of living specimens, will convey a better idea of the appearance of the lizard than any amount of written description. Coloured plates are very misleading, because all our reptiles have such a great extent of colour variation, and the most that any coloured plate can do, even if it be absolutely accurate, is to depict the appearance of one particular specimen. The observer is apt to get the impression therefrom that all lizards of the species represented are of that colour. For this reason, we have preferred to illustrate from photographs alone. "The general colour of the adult is brown or reddish above, with small darker and lighter spots; many specimens have a blackish vertebral streak and a dark lateral band edged with yellow. The under parts are orange to

[1] Gadow, *Amphibia and Reptiles*, p. 553.

red in the male, with conspicuous black spots; yellow or pale orange in the female, either without or with scanty black spots. The newly-born specimens are almost black. The males are slightly smaller than the females; males of a total length of 6 inches, and females 7 inches long, may be considered rather large specimens."[1] It is important to remember that the viviparous lizard is smaller than the sand lizard. Much confusion seems to prevail amongst field naturalists about the two species, and the sand lizard is constantly being reported from new localities, in Scotland for example, in mistake for the common viviparous lizard. The absolutely distinctive characters are few, but most specimens are clearly defined by their colours. If the distribution be compared, it will be at once noted that the sand lizard is very local and comparatively rare. In the common lizard no teeth are to be found on the palate bone, and in normal specimens there is a single post-nasal shield, and a single anterior loreal shield. The scales covering the dorsal surface are elongated and hexagonal, and indistinctly keeled as compared with those of the sand lizard. The general shape of the head is more flattened than in the rare species, and the snout more pointed. The ventral scales are arranged in from six to eight longitudinal rows: the marginal rows being the smallest; "the second series on each side from the median ventral line," the largest.[1] In these and other

[1] Gadow, *Amphibia and Reptiles*, p. 553.

COMMON LIZARD (FEMALE).

COMMON LIZARD (MALE).

[*Facing p.* 49.

lizards there are no glands in the skin, unless the femoral and pre-anal pores which occur in this and many other species are to be regarded as glands. These pores are found on the under-surface of the thighs, particularly in the males, and also in front of the anal opening. Those on the thigh of the common lizard number from nine to twelve. "Each of these organs perforates a scale and leads into a tubular invagination, which is lined with epidermal cells, the proliferation of which produces a horny yellowish débris, and this fills the tube and appears above the surface in the shape of a little cone."[1] The function of this excretion is not definitely ascertained, but possibly it is concerned in gratifying some sense-perception. Professor Cope remarks upon this: "The use of this substance is uncertain, but it is probably an important aid to the animal in maintaining its hold on smooth surfaces. Lizards which move on the ground rest much on the thighs, which are not elevated above the ground in many types, but serve as the principal point of contact from which they make their leaps. The same is true of some genera which leap among trees from branches and trunks. A similar secretion issues from the pre-anal scales in some Iguanidæ (*Liolæmus*, etc.), and in an African Lacertid a rudimentary structure of this character is found on many of the abdominal scales (*Poroidogaster*). An approximation to this structure I have seen on

[1] Gadow, *Amphibia and Reptiles*, p. 553.

the pre-anal scales of an adult male of *Sceloporus horridus* of Mexico. Here the epidermis is greatly thickened above the middle posterior part of the scale, so much so as to make a deep impression in the true skin, simulating a true pre-anal pore. I suspect that the nature of these structures is similar to that of corns in higher Vertebrata." [1]

The relative size, the colour, and the viviparous character of the common lizard, will be the points that the field naturalist will keep in mind as distinguishing this species from the sand lizard, not forgetting the wide distribution of the former compared with the very restricted distribution of the latter.

Haunts.—It has been noted that, as far as Europe is concerned, this lizard shows a preference for mountainous areas, but in England it will be found in flat districts as well as hilly. My own experience has been to see more specimens in dry sandy spots than in well-watered and greener places. Moors and commons and heaths seem to be its haunts particularly, as well as sandhills near the coast. I took half a dozen of these lizards one morning on the sand-heaps on the coast of Norfolk, near Stalham, where they scuttled across the sand from one stunted bush to another, or into tussocks of grass. I also saw a good many on a gorse-covered common in Dorset, so that they are not very particular as to the kind of

[1] Cope, *Crocodiles, Lizards, and Snakes*, p. 198.

THE COMMON LIZARD, *LACERTA VIVIPARA*

place they dwell in. Open country they certainly prefer to deep valleys and woods.

Habits.—Reptiles are frequently described as being sluggish and slow of movement. This is certainly not true of many lizards, and is very wide of the mark in the case of the viviparous lizard. A more difficult creature to catch it would be hard to mention. The pace at which one of these creatures will cross a piece of open ground to the nearest cover is simply astonishing, and almost defies capture by the hand. The observer sees the lizard first here, then there, and then not at all, and it is a hundred to one against finding it, unless it has sought the shelter of an isolated tuft of grass, from which it may be dislodged. Even then it is very difficult to see the little creature amongst the roots, and just as it is exposed and you are about to grasp it, like a flash it darts out and away to another more secure hiding-place. As to attempting to see the individual movements of the limbs it is a sheer impossibility. In fact, all the movements of this lizard are rapid. Feeding is carried out in desperate haste, as well as locomotion.

During the hot summer months they may be seen sunning themselves in the open, especially the gravid females, at which time, of course, their movements are more deliberate and less speedy, and therefore they are at this period more easily captured.

L. vivipara is said to be a good swimmer and to take readily to water. It is also stated that when the young are first born they remain with the parent for a time, and, like the adder, she has been credited with swallowing them for purposes of protection. Personally, I have never observed any indication of parental relationship in these lizards, either in nature or in captivity.

This lizard has a greater objection to being handled than either the slow-worm or the sand lizard; very hard it is to retain one in the hand without injury if it is attempting to wriggle out.

Sloughing occurs at intervals as in other lizards, it being somewhat rare to obtain a perfect slough in one piece (see page 39).

J. A. thus describes some habits of this lizard (*Newcastle Weekly Chronicle*, 1881):—

"Some years ago I remember being on a bird-nesting excursion in Belford Cragg. Seeing a bird flying about with food in its mouth, I concealed myself up the branches of a tall, thick holly-bush, and there waited quietly to see where the bird would go to feed its young. I had not sat more than a few minutes, when a small lizard crept out from the side of a stone and laid itself quietly down to bask in the sun's rays. It was presently joined by a second, and then a third, fourth, and fifth. I watched the motions of these little creatures for nearly an hour, and so interesting and amusing were they that I forgot to observe what became of the bird with the 'bait' in its mouth. Sometimes they would lie motionless, separated from each other by a few yards; then suddenly one would dart swiftly towards his neighbour, who, in turn, with equal agility, would avoid the attack; then a general darting to and fro, helter-skelter, would occur amongst the lot. Suddenly there was a pause, and all would lie still; then one would dart at some insect, secure it, and resume his vigils; then in a moment all was commotion again, a general darting here and there in all directions. Could not I secure one of these little lizards, thought I. But how was it to be done? The slightest movement on my part alarmed the whole, and they were all out of sight in an instant. In a short time they would return and resume their manœuvres. I thought

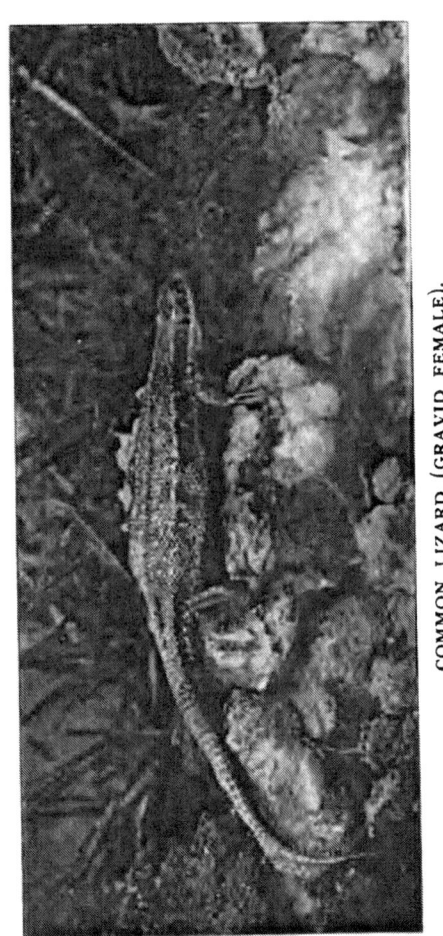

COMMON LIZARD (GRAVID FEMALE).
LACERTA VIVIPARA.

[*Facing p.* 52.

the best way to secure one was to overturn the stones under which they had taken shelter. Accordingly I began to turn over first one stone and then another, and after seeking for a considerable time, and turning over several stones under which I felt *sure* one at least had taken shelter, I was compelled to give up the search in despair, without getting a glimpse of the animals again. Such is the capacity of the lizard for keeping out of sight that it is next to impossible to capture it when once it gets among rough stones, grass, or heath ; and the rapidity with which it darts about on a surface of loose sand can only be likened to the movements of a dragon-fly on a pool of water."

Food.—The insects furnish the main food supply of this species. Flies of various kinds, blue-bottles, the small blue dragon-flies which abound in July in some places, June bugs, and beetles. In captivity meal worms are generally depended upon, and these the lizards take with evident satisfaction. An insect which ventures within seeing distance of the lizard is instantly captured and swallowed with great celerity. Caterpillars in their season are not despised, and they seem to vary the diet during successive months, doubtless as the different insects become more numerous. Miss Hopley found that her captive lizards took flies in the early summer only, and later on refused them ; and she hazards the opinion that the flies may be obnoxious when depositing their eggs. All her lizards refused centipedes, and ejected any if swallowed accidentally. Spiders they all took eagerly.

Reproduction.—As the specific name implies, the common lizard is viviparous or ovo-viviparous. The number of the family varies from six to twelve. The young burst the egg-membrane just after extrusion or within the mother; in the latter case, therefore, they are born quite free. No nest of any kind is made. The mother simply deposits the young upon the ground and leaves them to their own devices. As they have the perfect use of their limbs from the moment of birth, this apparent carelessness of the mother has no disadvantageous effect upon the young, who, in obedience to the dictates of hunger, very soon commence the search for small insects. These little ones, as already mentioned, are nearly black at first. In size they measure about an inch at birth, or a fraction less. Within a week they are actively engaged in feeding, but for the first few days they remain under leaves, and apparently subsist upon the remaining yolk from the egg, which has passed into the body. "Their first food consists of Aphides and similar tiny insects."[1]

Synonyms.—The various names by which this lizard is known are as follows:—

> The common lizard.
> The viviparous lizard.
> The scaly lizard.

In addition to the correct specific name of *L. vivipara*, the name *Zootoca vivipara* will be found in many writings applied to this species. The classification is given on page 101, and the specific scaling characters which distinguish it from the sand lizard are described in the chapter on "Specific Characters."

[1] Gadow, *Amphibia and Reptiles*, p. 554.

CHAPTER VII

THE SAND LIZARD, *LACERTA AGILIS*

DISTRIBUTION——DESCRIPTION——HAUNTS——HABITS——
FOOD——COLOUR VARIATION——REPRODUCTION.

Distribution.—The sand lizard, like the common lizard, is widely distributed in Europe, but must be regarded as an inhabitant of the plains rather than of the mountains. It is especially found, that is, in low-lying land. It occurs in Germany, Switzerland, Poland, the North of Russia, Siberia; but in the British Isles it is limited in its distribution to a few of the most southern counties. A good deal of confusion exists in the minds of field naturalists on this point, specimens of the common viviparous lizard frequently being recorded as sand lizards, the reason for this mistake undoubtedly being that the great range of colour variation seen in the latter is not sufficiently well known. It is too generally assumed by those who are not familiar with the appearance of both species that any light brown or sandy-coloured lizard must be a sand lizard, which is far from actually the case. A careful examination of the two species together will render the distinctions quite obvious; but a large number of field naturalists never see a sand lizard, owing to its limited distribution, and hence are liable, on encountering an unfamiliar colour variation in the common lizard, to erroneously put the specimen down as *Lacerta agilis*. The distribution of the sand lizard in this country is practically that of the smooth snake (*Coronella austriaca*), namely, restricted localities in Dorset, Hants, and Surrey, rarely anywhere else.

The sand lizard is not very rare on some Dorset heaths, being found especially in the neighbourhood of Poole. It is perhaps as common in parts of Surrey, but is everywhere very local in its distribution. It has been stated to occur in Berkshire, but the evidence is not good, though it is very interesting to remember that twenty years ago the smooth snake (*C. austriaca*) was also found in that county, where it has recently reappeared.[1] When we consider the close connection between these two reptiles, it is just possible that *L. agilis* once inhabited Berkshire, and that the same causes which led to the extermination of its enemy, the smooth snake, also had an influence in its own distribution. At any rate, it is not found there to-day. Coming to other counties, this species has often been recorded in places where there is no doubt

[1] "Reappearance of the Smooth Snake in Berkshire," *The Field Naturalist's Quarterly*, August 1903.

SAND LIZARD (MALE).

SAND LIZARD (FEMALE).

[*Facing p.* 56.

THE SAND LIZARD, *LACERTA AGILIS* 57

it never existed, on the authority of more or less incompetent naturalists. Thus Mr. Forrest was led to include the species in the *Vertebrate Fauna of Shropshire*, not from his own observation, but on the authority of others who asserted they had seen it. After this otherwise excellent book was published, Mr. Forrest, having his doubts raised as to the accuracy of these observations, conferred with G. A. Boulenger upon the matter, and in a letter to myself on the matter, he says, " as a result of this conference I have come to the conclusion that all these observers were mistaken, and that all the lizards in Shropshire which were said to be sand lizards belonged to the *L. vivipara* species." No doubt this is really the case. Personally, I have had the sand lizard reported to me from Scotland (Ayrshire), but I never could get the specimen forwarded for inspection, so upon this record, too, the gravest doubt must rest.

The neighbourhood of Bournemouth has been one of the districts where the sand lizard frequented ; and F. G. Aflalo says, " I have dug it up in this state (*i.e.* in hibernation) near Bournemouth, where it is very common." [1]

The general statement may be made, therefore, that the sand lizard is practically confined to those counties south of the Thames, and is found particularly in Surrey, Hampshire, and Dorset.

Are there no reliable records of the occurrence of

[1] *British Vertebrates*, p. 302.

this species in the northern counties of England? To answer that question we cannot do better than quote a communication to *The Zoologist* of September 1901, by Mr. T. A. Coward, the well-known Cheshire ornithologist. We give the communication *in extenso*, as it covers the ground, and from it my readers can gather the position of the matter. It is as follows:—

"THE SAND LIZARD IN THE NORTH OF ENGLAND.

"In the recent volume of the *Cambridge Natural History* on 'Amphibia and Reptiles,' Dr. Hans Gadow says that the sand lizard (*L. agilis*, Linn.) 'is absent in Ireland and Scotland, while in England it is restricted to the southern half'; and a similar statement is made by Mr. Boulenger in the Hampshire volume of the *Victoria History of the Counties of England*. The reputed sand lizards, frequently reported from northern counties, generally prove, on investigation, to be large examples of the common lizard (*L. vivipara*). This, however, is not the case in Lancashire, and, I believe, in Cheshire, for on the coast sandhills the true sand lizard was formerly common, and may even yet occur in places where the sandhills are unreclaimed. Lancashire naturalists of the old school knew the sand lizard well, but, as questions of geographical distribution did not greatly interest them, there are few records left beyond the bare fact that the species was common. There are, however, specimens in the Warrington Museum, whose identity Mr.

Boulenger has confirmed, which were captured at Southport and Formby, on the Lancashire coast. In Mr. Isaac Byerley's *Fauna of Liverpool*, published in 1856, the sand lizard is described as occurring 'on the sandhills from West Kirby to New Brighton' (in Cheshire). 'At Seaforth, Crosby, and elsewhere' (in Lancashire). Mr. W. D. Roebuck states (*Naturalist*, 1884-85, p. 258) that, after examining specimens sent to him from various North of England localities, and finding that they were only 'lightly coloured specimens of the viviparous lizard,' he did not believe in the existence of the true *L. agilis* so far north, until Mr. G. T. Porritt procured him a couple of specimens from the Southport sandhills, which he 'at once saw were unmistakably referable to that species.' He adds: 'Mr. Porritt tells me these lizards swarm on the sandhills at Southport, where he has frequently seen them sparkling in the sun with a glistening emerald-green, and sometimes almost golden, brightness.' The late Thomas Alcock, in his pamphlet on the *Natural History of the Coast of Lancashire* (1887), also speaks of the sand lizard at Southport, where he says it was 'formerly plentiful on the isolated group of sandhills at the north end of the town. Hesketh Park, however, now occupies the best part of this locality.' In 1862 and 1865 he captured and received a number of examples from this place. Mr. H. O. Forbes, in the *British Association Handbook* for 1896, says, on the authority of Mr. Linnæus Greening, of Warrington, 'Common; Wallasey, Southport, and Formby sandhills.' The Cheshire locality is included on the strength of specimens which were shown to Mr. Greening by the late C. S. Gregson, who stated that he had obtained them at Wallasey. The sandhills between West Kirby and New Brighton were of the same character as those extending along the Lancashire coast from Liverpool to the mouth of the Ribble, and it is a generally accepted theory that the river Mersey, within geologically recent times, used to empty itself into the sea considerably to the west of its present mouth; so that at one time the Wallasey coast-line was north of the river. The spread of the suburban residential districts round Liverpool, the growth of seaside resorts, such as Hoylake and West Kirby, and the formation of golf links all along the coast have destroyed a large portion of these sandhills; but there are considerable stretches in both counties where the lizard may still exist. The sand lizard is not known in Cumberland or Westmoreland, and, although many miles of the North Wales coast, from the mouth of the Dee westward, are, or were, similar in character to the Cheshire shores, I know of no record of the sand lizard from the Principality. The evidence therefore shows that *L. agilis*, generally considered to be only an inhabitant of some of the southern counties, occurs in the north, on a strip of sandhills bordering the Irish Sea, from the mouth

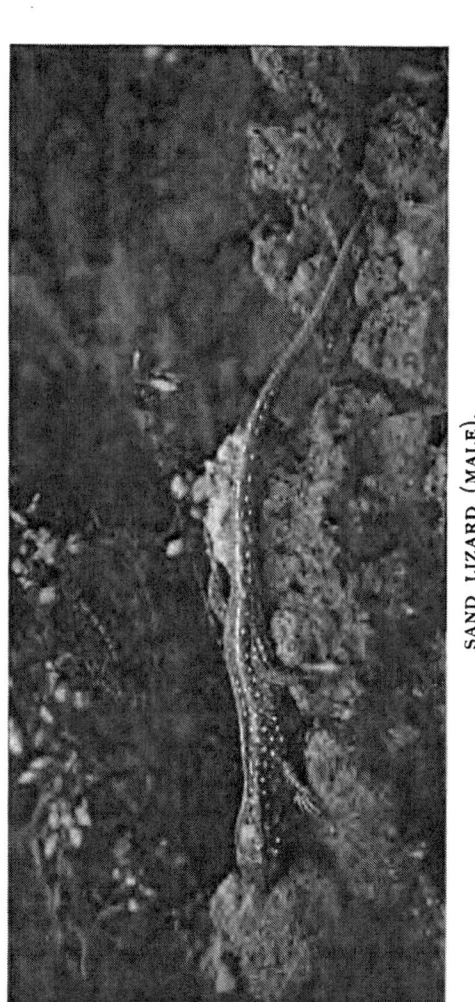

SAND LIZARD (MALE).
LACERTA AGILIS.

[*Facing p.* 60.

THE SAND LIZARD, *LACERTA AGILIS* 61

of the Ribble to the outskirts of Liverpool, and, unless Byerley's and Gregson's specimens were incorrectly localised, on the Cheshire shore from West Kirby to New Brighton."

Description.—A glance at the photographs of this species will convey the correct impression that the sand lizard is larger and of heavier build than the viviparous species. Associated with this is the fact that *L. agilis*, in spite of its specific name, is less agile than the smaller common form. It possesses granular nodes over the eye, and teeth upon the palate bone, the latter an important distinction between the two lizards. A comparison of the scales on the body will reveal that in the sand lizard these are more numerous across from one side of the back to the other, and also that the individual scales are smaller and evidently keeled. On the dorsal aspect these scales are more rounded or irregular than in *L. vivipara*, where we saw they were hexagonal and elongated. In colour there is the greatest variety, which is responsible for much of the confusion between the two species. Dr. Gadow describes it thus :—" The colouration is subject to much variation, local as well as individual. As a rule, the sand lizard gives the impression of being striped longitudinally, the striation being caused by rows of dark and white spots and patches along the sides of the back, flanks, and tail. In the male a more or less pronounced green, in the female brown and grey are the prevailing ground-colours. A typically coloured male during the breeding season is grass-green on the sides and suffused with green on the yellow under parts; the sides are dotted with black, with whitish eye-spots. The under parts are spotted with black. The adult female is brown or grey above, with large dark brown, white-centred spots, which are arranged in three rows on each side. The under parts are cream-coloured, with or without black specks. The young are grey-brown above, with white, black-edged spots; the under parts are whitish."[1] A careful description such as the above shows how impossible it is to convey an accurate impression of the colour of this species by a coloured plate. Comparing the shields with those of the viviparous lizard we find that the sand lizard has, as a rule, two anterior loreal shields in place of the one in the smaller lizard, these two along with the single post-nasal shield making a triangle. The average size of the male sand lizard is about 7½ inches, the female being a little larger, 8 inches or rather more. Again, it is to be observed that the tail in the male sex is relatively longer than in the female, in the latter it is less than one-half of the entire length of the lizard. The tail is cylindrical, and covered by a number of rings of scales, these scales being more elongated than those on the dorsum. These annulations have a distinct relation to the position where fracture of the tail is apt to occur, a point which is dealt with later.

[1] Gadow, *Amphibia and Reptiles*, p. 554.

SAND LIZARD (FEMALE, GRAVID, SHORT TAIL). [*Facing p.* 62.

Haunts.—The popular name of sand lizard in this case appears to rest upon a good foundation, sandy districts it undoubtedly affects. There is good reason for this in connection with the two physiological processes in this species of reproduction and hibernation. The warmth of the sand assists the former—for in this case the eggs are deposited early, while the ease with which it can burrow in loose sandy soil assists in hibernation. Sunshine is a much more necessary condition of life to the sand lizard than to the slow-worm, hence the former keeps to the open and undisturbed sandy heaths and commons, with sunny banks on which to bask. Much of its life is passed underground, and on the slightest approach of cold it retreats from exposure to air. But on bright warm days the sunniest spot in its local habitat will find the sand lizard deriving all the heat it can for its cold-blooded system from the sun. It is a dweller in plains rather than mountains.

Habits.—There is always the danger in attempting to give an account of the character and disposition of an animal, that its behaviour in captivity, *i.e.* under artificial conditions, is assumed to be identical with that in the natural wild state. Further, we know that in some reptiles, the adder for example,[1] the effect of captivity upon the character is very marked. But the great difficulty has to be faced that it is practically impossible to watch some creatures in

[1] *Field Naturalist's Quarterly*, vol. i. No. 1.

nature, and in no case could that difficulty be much greater than in the sand lizard, except perhaps in fish. The sand lizard simply refuses to allow itself to be studied out of doors, at anyrate at close quarters. So that we are forced to gain our impressions from their behaviour in vivaria, where the conditions of existence are made as natural as possible. It is well that this should be frankly stated, because the impressions thus gained may not be perfectly accurate if applied to the wild reptile. Even then the difficulty is not ended, for various observers have recorded the most diverse opinions of the disposition of the sand lizard. Assuming that all these recorders were truthful, which doubtless they were, the conclusion to be arrived at is that the disposition in this lizard is a greatly varying one. Some are snappish, others docile; some refuse to feed, others feed readily; some inoffensive, others pugnacious; and so on. Miss Hopley had a male *L. agilis* which "at once displayed an aggressive viciousness of temper that would be deplorable were it not ridiculous. He not only turned to bite whenever approached, but held on to the finger so persistently as to be carried about the house on exhibition thus pendent. His feeble little jaws could, of course, inflict no injury; therefore, his spiteful efforts to grip the harder whenever touched, as he thus hung, were simply laughable, reminding one of the fly on the bull's horn, only lacking the fly's polite apologies. If he happened to grip a fleshy part of the hand, you might afterwards almost count the number of his teeth, from the two little rows of indentations, like a V. The skin was never penetrated. To do him justice this temper lasted only a few days; and very soon he was the tamest of the family, which, at that time, consisted of himself and two ladies *agilis*, and five of *L. zootoca.*"[1] Here is a case in point, where the lizard at first showed signs of a disposition which afterwards disappeared. Is it not just possible that the whole exhibition of apparent temper was really due to abject fear and fright in the new surroundings? One can quite understand the reptile hanging on to the finger "like grim death," while being carried about pendent, not necessarily from innate viciousness, but from an instinctive knowledge that if he let go he would fall and hurt himself. Lizards are extremely timid creatures until they become accustomed to their owners, and thus exhibit all sorts of curious traits when first made captive. Whether their subsequent good behaviour, when they have settled down to their vivarium life, is their real mood, or merely an acquiescence in the inevitable, my readers must judge for themselves.

Food.—As in the case of the viviparous lizard, insects of various kinds are the main diet of this species in nature. In captivity, as hinted above, some specimens refuse to feed, but most take food without difficulty.

Colour variation.—When describing the sand lizard

[1] i.e. *Lacerta vivipara.*

the various colours which are met with were mentioned. It need only be stated here that a large series of specimens will show a great range of colour variation, and it is only by examining such a series that the student of lizards can become familiar with all the differences which the species may show. The general impression will be gained that the males have more green about them than the females, the latter of which include the browner types. Thus sex evidently plays a part in the production of the varying colours, and the other factors concerned will be studied in a later chapter.

Reproduction.—The sand lizard is the only lizard of the mainland of Great Britain which is oviparous or an egg-layer. In this respect it agrees with the green lizard and the wall lizard of the Channel Isles, and with one of our snakes, namely, the ring-snake. Pairing takes place in England in May or June, according to the particular kind of spring weather in vogue. The eggs are deposited some four weeks or so later, in July, to the number of eight, frequently five, six, or seven. Some observers state that as many as a dozen are sometimes deposited. The female simply makes a depression in the sand, and leaves the eggs to hatch out by the aid of the heat of the sun and moisture. If the habitat be not in sandy ground, the eggs will be placed under leaves, earth, or débris. The egg-membrane is thin, but of firm consistence, having a parchment-like appearance.

THE SAND LIZARD, *LACERTA AGILIS*

Enemies.—Whatever the enemies of the sand lizard may be in other lands, by far the most important and interesting from the present point of view is the smooth snake (*Coronella austriaca*). We have seen that the distribution of these two reptiles in England is practically identical, and *L. agilis* seems to be the one meal which *Coronella* delights in above all others. An average-sized sand lizard is a large morsel for a snake only 2 feet long to manipulate, but it is astonishing what the serpent jaw is capable of in the direction of swallowing. When in the gullet of the snake the lizard will occupy the whole length of that organ, and if swallowed head-first in the usual way, the head of the lizard just reaches the entrance of the stomach at the end of the swallowing process. Digestion there takes place progressively as the lizard passes into the stomach, the part in the œsophagus being left undigested, so that one sometimes finds in the snake a lizard half digested, the intact part being that still in the gullet.

The sand lizard is also preyed upon by the adder (*Vipera berus*).

CHAPTER VIII

THE GREEN LIZARD, *LACERTA VIRIDIS*

DISTRIBUTION—DESCRIPTION—HAUNTS—HABITS—
FOOD—REPRODUCTION.

Distribution.—A further word of explanation is necessary to account for this species being introduced into a book which purports to deal only with British lizards. It is not at all a question of the evidence concerning the capture of this or that specimen in this or that locality, or the further argument thereupon as to whether these captured green lizards are to be regarded as indigenous. As far as England is concerned, *Lacerta viridis* is not, and never has been, an indigenous species, and the capture of a few specimens under circumstances which seem to point to their being so, merely indicates that out of the very large number that are kept by dealers and as vivarium pets, some few every now and then manage to make their escape from captivity. The same thing has occurred with a tortoise, but it was not therefore seriously urged that land tortoises were to be regarded

THE GREEN LIZARD, *LACERTA VIRIDIS* 69

as indigenous British reptiles. The real reason why the green lizard finds a place here is simply because according to the "County and Vice-County Divisions of the British Isles" (for biological purposes), the Channel Islands form one division; and as the green lizard and the wall lizard are both indigenous in those islands, it has been necessary for the sake of uniformity and accuracy to include both species in this book.[1]

Distribution.—In Europe the distribution of the green lizard may be said to be mainly in the centre and southern portions of that continent. It is fairly common in France. I recently had a specimen of the asp (*Vipera aspis*) sent to me from the Gironde district which contained a full-grown green lizard in its gullet. It is also found in Italy, the south of Switzerland, Sicily, Greece, Poland, Austria, Barbary, and the Morea. It is not indigenous to England, Scotland, or Ireland, but is so in the Channel Isles. It is essentially an inhabitant of warm and temperate climates, and hence is found to be common in those areas washed by the Mediterranean.

The belief which many people in the south of England have, that the green lizard is truly indigenous, has been supported, or possibly originated, by a remark of Gilbert White's in the *Natural History of Selborne*.

---

[1] This sheet was issued by Alexander Somerville, B.Sc., F.L.S., after consultation with most of the leading naturalists in this country; in it the whole country is mapped out into divisions according to natural boundaries. It is most valuable to field naturalists in tracing out distribution.

It occurs in Letter XXII., and runs thus:—"It is a satisfaction to me to find that a green lizard has actually been procured for you in Devonshire; because it corroborates my discovery, which I made many years ago, of the same sort, on a sunny sandbank near Farnham, in Surrey. I am well acquainted with the south hams of Devonshire; and can suppose that district, from its southerly situation, to be a proper habitation for such animals in their best colours." There is not much in the paragraph to throw accurate light upon the source of this specimen; Pennant did not even take it himself, it was "procured" for him. The context, however, clearly shows that both White and Pennant understood the specimen to have been a wild specimen captured in the open. The association of the incident with White's own discovery at Farnham probably reveals the true nature of the lizard, since, as we have seen, Farnham is one of the localities frequented by the sand lizard (*L. agilis*). The green colour of the specimen was the feature that specially attracted the attention of both these observers, and that, as we have already noted, is a prominent characteristic of the males of the sand lizard species. Both the specimen procured for Pennant and that seen by White at Farnham were doubtless sand lizards. White's remark concerning the suitability of Devonshire for the requirements of *L. viridis* may be quite correct, but it is of no value, since it is a common occurrence in nature to find the absence of species in places apparently well adapted for them. That White was not very familiar with the green lizard is evident from the first sentence of the very next letter (Letter XXIII.), where he says: "It is not improbable that the Guernsey lizard and our green lizard may be specifically the same; all that I know is, that, when some years ago many Guernsey lizards were turned loose in Pembroke College garden, in the University of Oxford, they lived a great while, and seemed to enjoy themselves very well, but never bred." Indeed, the naturalist of Selborne appears to have given very little attention to the local reptiles, if one may judge from the paucity of his references to them.

Then, of course, green lizards are not uncommonly found as escaped captives. I am not aware to what extent they were kept as vivarium pets in the days when Gilbert White wrote, but nowadays a very large number of people have vivaria with them in captivity, and like all lizards they are quick to take the opportunity of a door left open, so that the real wonder is that not more specimens are thus encountered. I know lizard lovers, too, who, desirous of introducing such a graceful and beautiful creature, have deliberately set free some specimens in their own locality, but I am not aware of any of these having been recaptured. The conclusion is absolutely certain, however, that *L. viridis* is not an indigenous lizard to the mainland of Great Britain, although in time, if sufficient are introduced and set free, it may succeed in establishing itself in some counties. From the field naturalist's point of view such a consummation is devoutly to be wished, as it would make a handsome addition to our all too scanty reptile fauna.

Description.—The green lizard is considerably larger than any of the other lizards encountered in the British Isles, with the exception of the slow-worm, which indeed reaches as great a length, but is not nearly so bulky a creature. The average size of the adult may be put at 12 to 15 inches, though a good number of specimens exceed this measurement. The males, as in most other lizards, are larger than the females, very large males reaching a length of 16 or 17 inches. Here again, the observer must be careful to see whether the tail is intact before coming to a conclusion as to the total length, for the tail is responsible for the greater part of the total length, almost three-quarters of it in very long males.

The predominating colour, as the name implies, is green. This is particularly upon the upper surface, and therefore the colour most readily seen. It shades off into yellow on the belly, the intermediate part, or the lateral aspect, being greenish yellow.

Other colours are found in special parts of the body. If the specimen be a male in the breeding season, the throat will exhibit a bluish tinge. The prevailing green of the back will often be mottled with black specks, or yellow spots. Often, too, a decided brown

GREEN LIZARD.
LACERTA VIRIDIS.

[Facing p. 72.

THE GREEN LIZARD, *LACERTA VIRIDIS*

colour will be noticed. As in other reptiles, *age* has an influence on the colouring. In this species it affects specially the stripes on the sides, which in the young ones are yellow. These disappear in the older males, but are persistent in some of the adult females.

There is a distinct semicircular collar on the neck. The eyelids are prominent, the head flattened, and the snout rather pointed. The post-nasal shields are generally two in number, one overlapping the other. The head shields are large, the scales on the back small, the ventral scales in longitudinal rows, the scales on the tail elongated and hexagonal, again arranged in annular fashion. The transition from the small body scales to the long hexagonal tail scales is abrupt, and the tail very gradually tapers to a very fine point. These characters can be made out in the illustrations, and the several species may be compared to show their respective prominence.

Haunts and Habits. — Since it is only in the Channel Islands that we have to deal with the green lizard as a British species, it will suffice to say that, as far as its haunts are concerned, it prefers rocky ground at a somewhat high altitude.

In its habits it is mainly terrestrial, but not exclusively so, as it has frequently been observed to climb trees, especially when endeavouring to elude a pursuer. Dr. Gadow states that in these circumstances, if hard pressed, the green lizard will take tremendous leaps down to the ground, curiously enough without sustaining the fracture of the tail which under some other conditions occurs with great ease. This lizard is another example of a reptile which is anything but slow and sluggish in its movements; indeed, the very opposite is the truth, it is extremely quick and agile. In captivity it has been found by some to do badly, whilst others have found no difficulty in keeping it. It certainly does not seem to thrive after a year or so, possibly the artificial hibernation is not satisfactory. It soon becomes accustomed to its owner and free from all fear.

Food.—As usual insects of one kind or another are largely partaken of. Butterflies are said to be a favourite diet. Worms also, and, according to Dr. Gadow, snails, are eaten. In a specimen the author has from Gironde, the stomach was nearly full of a species of black beetle. The lizard itself was from the gullet of a smooth snake, so that the snake, the lizard, and the beetles, formed a striking object-lesson on the struggle for existence in nature. What the beetles contained in the way of food was not ascertained.

Reproduction.—After the green lizards emerge from the winter hibernation, the males fight amongst themselves a good deal previous to pairing with the females, which takes place in the spring months. After fertilisation, the eggs are partially developed in the female oviducts, where they are carried for four weeks. They are then deposited in situations suitable

GREEN LIZARD: VENTRAL SURFACE.

[Facing p. 74.

THE GREEN LIZARD, *LACERTA VIRIDIS*

for further development with the aid of warmth, and the young are hatched out in another four weeks, so that the whole period of gestation is eight weeks. The young, or at any rate the eggs deposited, are usually from eight to ten in number. They have yellow lateral lines, which, as we saw, persist in some of the females in adult life. With regard to the question of the mother exercising any watch over the eggs, or giving any other sign of interest, Miss Hopley says: "Mr. Jenner Weir told me of one (a green lizard, that is) in his possession, who displayed not only vigilance and care for her eggs, but considerable wiliness in secreting them. The spot where she had laid them being discovered, she being there, hastily retreated, but presently returned and scratched the peat over them till hidden by a little mound; then continued day after day to visit the spot and bask on the mound; but, as if conscious of being watched, would never do anything to betray the place while anyone was near."[1] The whole question of parental relationship is a very interesting one in reptiles, as they seem to be on the border line of those vertebrates which give indications of its evolution. *A priori* one would expect to find it appearing first in those animals which brought forth their young alive, rather than in oviparous creatures such as the green lizard.

[1] C. Hopley, *British Reptiles*, p. 92.

CHAPTER IX

THE WALL LIZARD, *LACERTA MURALIS*

DISTRIBUTION——HABITS——DESCRIPTION——CHARACTERS COMMON TO THE FAMILY.

WE have already explained why it is that the green lizard has found a place in a work on British species, and it is for the same reasons that the wall lizard, *Lacerta muralis*, must be here included. The one cannot be regarded as a British species unless the other be also so regarded, since it is simply a question of the inclusion or omission of the Channel Islands in the area denominated British. Since we include these islands in our faunal divisions, both these species, on that ground alone, become British.

Whilst it is necessary, for the sake of consistency and uniformity, to do this, the fact remains that the average field naturalist in this country has but a nominal acquaintance with the wall lizard; and since it will not come under his observation in field work, unless he pays a visit to its habitat in the Channel Islands or elsewhere, it is not necessary to treat it

WALL LIZARD.

WALL LIZARD (MALE).
LACERTA MURALIS.

[*Facing p.* 77.

in the same detail as in the case of the other species.

Distribution.—The wall lizard is a very common species in the countries of South Europe, as well as across the Mediterranean in Northern Africa. It is also common in Asia Minor. To the north its distribution extends as far as the more southern portion of Germany, and into Belgium. Dr. Gadow states that in the Iberian Peninsula it is found at an altitude of 5000 or 6000 feet above the level of the sea. Speaking generally, the distribution of this species may be said to be chiefly in those countries bordering upon the Mediterranean.

Description and Habits.—The average length of the wall lizard is from 6 to 8 inches, so that it is one of the smaller species. "This graceful little creature is easily recognised by the series of granules between the supra-ocular and supra-ciliary scales, and usually by having only six rows of ventral scales. The great variety in colouration has given rise to the establishment of many races, varieties, and subspecies. In the typical forms the upper parts are brown or greyish, with blackish spots or streaks, sometimes with a bronzy-greenish sheen. The under parts are white, yellow, pink, or red, either uniform or, especially in the males, with large black spots. The lateral rows of ventral shields are frequently blue. The colour-varieties are almost endless. One of the most noteworthy is that described as var. *cærulea* by Eimer;

this, confined to the Faraglione Rocks, near Capri, is blackish above, like the rock, and sapphire-blue below.[1] Similarly coloured specimens, var. *lilfordi*, occur on some of the rocky islets of the Balearic Isles.

"The wall lizard deserves its name, since in the Mediterranean countries there is scarcely a wall on which these active lizards do not bask or run up and down; often head downwards, in search of insects. They are oviparous. The hibernation is short and not very deep, since these lizards can sometimes be seen basking on sunny winter days before their regular appearance in the early spring."[2]

As its specific name implies, the wall lizard belongs to the same family—the Lacertidæ—as the green lizard, the common viviparous lizard, and the sand lizard. The slow-worm is the only British species which is not of this family. This family of Lacertidæ, or the True Lizards, as they are called, comprises "nearly twenty genera, with about one hundred species, and is typical of the Old World, being found in Europe, Asia, Africa, but not in Madagascar, nor in the Australian region. They are most abundant in Africa. Their northern limit coincides fairly closely with the limit of the permanently frozen underground. All the Lacertidæ live upon animal food, chiefly insects, and, after them, worms and snails; but the larger lizards take what they can master, fre-

---

[1] Boulenger, *British Museum Catalogue.*
[2] Gadow, *Amphibia and Reptiles*, pp. 557, 558.

WALL LIZARD.

WALL LIZARD.

[*Facing p.* 78.

quently other lizards, and even younger members of their own kind. Many of them love sugar, which they lick, and all require water. They are all terrestrial, preferring, according to their kind, such localities as yield them their particular food. Sunshine and warmth make a marvellous change in the same individual, which on dull, rainy, or cold days lies in its hole, or shows only sluggish movements. Their sense of locality is great, or rather each individual inhabits one place of which it knows every nook and corner, cranny, tree, and bush. It has its favourite hole to sleep in, a stone, the branch of a tree, or a wall to bask upon, and when disturbed or chased it makes with unerring swiftness for a safe spot to retire into. The same lizard, when once driven away from its own locality, seems to lose all its presence of mind, flounders about, and is comparatively easily caught. Most lizards are extremely curious, although shy, and this state of their mind can be made use of by those who want to catch them without injury, and, above all, without getting the animal minus the brittle tail. This safe way of catching lizards consists in taking a thin rod with a running noose of thread at the end, in drawing the latter over the lizard's head, and then raising it. The little creature does not mind the rod in the least; on the contrary, it watches it carefully, and often makes for the thread. The boys in Southern Italy have improved upon and simplified this mode of catching lizards by bending the end of a wisp of grass into a noose, and covering the latter over with a thin film of saliva. The shiny film, like a soap-bubble, is sure to excite the curiosity of the creature. The late Professor Eimer refers to this practice as carried out by the children of two thousand years ago, and he sagaciously explains that the beautiful statue of the so-called Apollo Sauroctonos represents a boy who is in the act of noosing the little lizard on the tree." [1]

Field naturalists who wish to pursue their study of lizards beyond the limited lizard fauna of Great Britain, cannot do better than read Dr. Gadow's book, from which we have quoted the above passages.

The general appearance and attitudes of *L. muralis* may be best appreciated from the illustrations, which are from photographs of living specimens.

[1] Gadow, *Amphibia and Reptiles*, pp. 551-553.

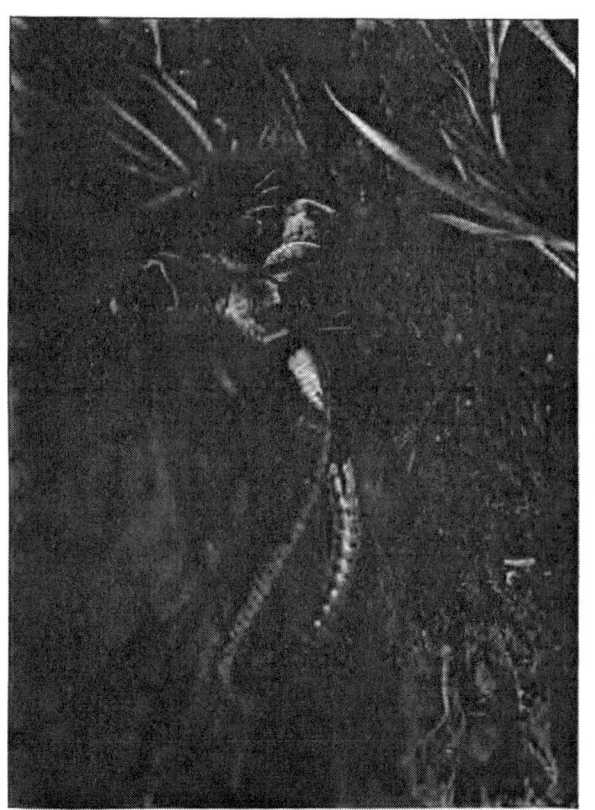

WALL LIZARD.
(*Showing fight.*)

[*Facing p.* 80.

CHAPTER X

THE SPECIFIC CHARACTERS OF BRITISH LIZARDS

TERMINOLOGY OF HEAD SCALES—SPECIFIC SCALING OF THE THREE SPECIES—CLASSIFICATION OF BRITISH SPECIES.

THE average field naturalist is not as a rule very interested in questions of minute structure and details of classification, unless he be a botanist or an entomologist. He is generally satisfied with being able to distinguish an adder from a ring-snake without troubling to learn the particular scaling arrangements which are characteristic of the species. And this state of knowledge or ignorance will be found to be specially applicable to the group of reptiles, the lizards as well as the snakes. If one inquires from the field worker—as the present writer has frequently done—why it is that the specific characters of our reptiles are so neglected, the reply given is that none of the semi-popular books which deal with the fauna of this country explain how those characters are arrived at, or the meanings of the descriptive terms used for each type. Whether the excuse is a good one or not, the charge is a perfectly true one, and the field worker, to a certain extent at any rate, is not to be blamed. It would, however, be inexcusable in a book dealing with lizards alone not to try and make this matter clear to the learner,—firstly, because it is an aspect that he ought to be familiar with; and secondly, because, unless he does know it, he cannot tell a typical specimen from an abnormal variation. If all field workers were quite familiar with the typical scale arrangements of our snakes and lizards, we should very soon be in possession of a far greater amount of information as to their variations than is obtainable at present. Every specimen captured by a member of a field club should be carefully examined to see whether it presents any deviation from the normal in scaling, and if it does, the record should be incorporated in the club transactions and sent to one of the zoological journals.

The present chapter, then, is an attempt to make clear to the beginner, what is regarded by most field workers as the uninteresting and rather mysterious question of scaling arrangements of species. As a matter of fact, once the *type* of a species is thoroughly learnt, it becomes a matter of the greatest interest to discover the variations from that type, and the technical terms which are unavoidable in this connection can be mastered with a few minutes' close application. After following out the diagrammatic representation of the relative positions of the various head scales (p. 86), the reader should endeavour to draw it himself from memory, so as to familiarise himself with the position of each scale. Then he should turn to the description of the specific scaling characters of each species and construct for himself a line drawing of the head of each species. This is even more important in the snakes than in the lizards, for the field naturalist who is familiar with the scaling of the heads of the adder and the ring-snake, can identify a specimen from the head alone, and is not misled by any considerations of size or colour. Whether this is the best possible manner that could be devised for classification, and whether weight should not be given to other characters more than it is, are questions which need not concern us here; the point is, that scaling arrangements are specific characters, and as such should be known by every field naturalist.

It is quite possible that originally the scales which cover the bodies of lizards were all alike, but a glance at one of the lizards of the present day will show that considerable differentiation has taken place between the scales of one part of the body and those of another. The scales of the head, back, limbs, and belly, have become different in shape, and in *type of arrangement*. For this reason those who have been responsible for making classifications of reptiles have found it best to take these as their guide. That is to say, the scaling becomes of the greatest importance in the distinction of one species from another, and of one genus from another. Some of the scales have become much larger than others, probably from fusion of the original small ones. Thus on the top of the head will be found some scales larger than those of the back, and of a different shape. As it is necessary for purposes of accurate description to give these larger scales or *head shields* definite names, they have been named from the particular positions they fill on the head, *e.g.* nasal shield. These various names must now be studied.

THE TERMINOLOGY OF THE HEAD SCALES.

In describing the head of any reptile we distinguish three aspects or surfaces. Two of these are visible when the lizard is in the natural attitude on the ground, the third only when lifted off the ground. First of all we have the upper aspect, that of the top of the head, the vertex or dorsal aspect. Secondly, there is the side view of the mouth and eyes, or the lateral aspect. These are the two ordinarily visible. Thirdly, there is the under surface of the head, that of the chin and throat, or the ventral aspect. On each of these surfaces are scales or shields arranged in a definite manner for each species, and named either after their position with regard to other parts of the head, or after some of the cranial bones which they cover.

These shields vary immensely in different species, some having more than others. In order to understand the general principle of their terminology, it is necessary to take an instance of a head which exhibits all the scales or shields which have special names. Such a typical head is shown in the illustrations here given. We shall see later which of these shields are present, and which are wanting in our indigenous lizards.

We restrict our description to those shields only which are most important for purposes of specific distinction, the rest may be disregarded by the field naturalist.

The three surfaces of the head must be taken in turn.

1. THE VERTEX.

The shields which claim attention on the top of the head are the following:—

> (a) The frontal; (b) the parietal; (c) the fronto-parietal; (d) the pre-frontal; (e) the inter-parietal; (f) the inter-nasal; (g) the inter-fronto-nasal; (h) the supra-ocular; (i) the occipital; (j) the temporal.

In addition to these, portions of the rostral shield, and of the nasal shields, may be visible from above; the former, however, is, strictly speaking, anterior—not superior, and the latter belong more to the lateral or side view.

Of those which are actually on the top of the head, the most important are the frontal, the parietals, the supra-ocular, and the pre-frontals.

These are the most constant in their presence and arrangement, and are always looked for first.

The most conspicuous is often the frontal, a large polygonal shield in the centre of the top of the head, a single shield in the middle line, which is easily recognised (F.). Immediately in front of this, anteriorly that is, are some smaller shields whose number and arrangement will be found to vary considerably, they are called from their position relative to the frontal, the pre-frontal shields (PF.). The part of the head behind the frontal is the parietal region. The two largest shields here, one on either side of the middle line, are the parietal shields (P.). Sometimes these parietals are in contact with the posterior border of the frontal, in other cases—as represented in the diagram—they are separated from the frontal by smaller shields, which are therefore termed the fronto-parietal shields. Further, if the two parietal shields are themselves separated from each other by a shield in the middle line, this will naturally be called the inter-parietal shield (IP.). Directly behind the parietal shields is a smaller one, which is the occipital shield (O.); while more to the side of the parietals but still posterior, are the temporal shields (T.).

We have thus disposed of the shields in front of and behind the large central frontal shield; there remains still the large shield found on either side of the frontal, which since it lies immediately above the eye region, is termed the supra-ocular (SO.).

TYPICAL LIZARD'S HEAD: DORSAL ASPECT.

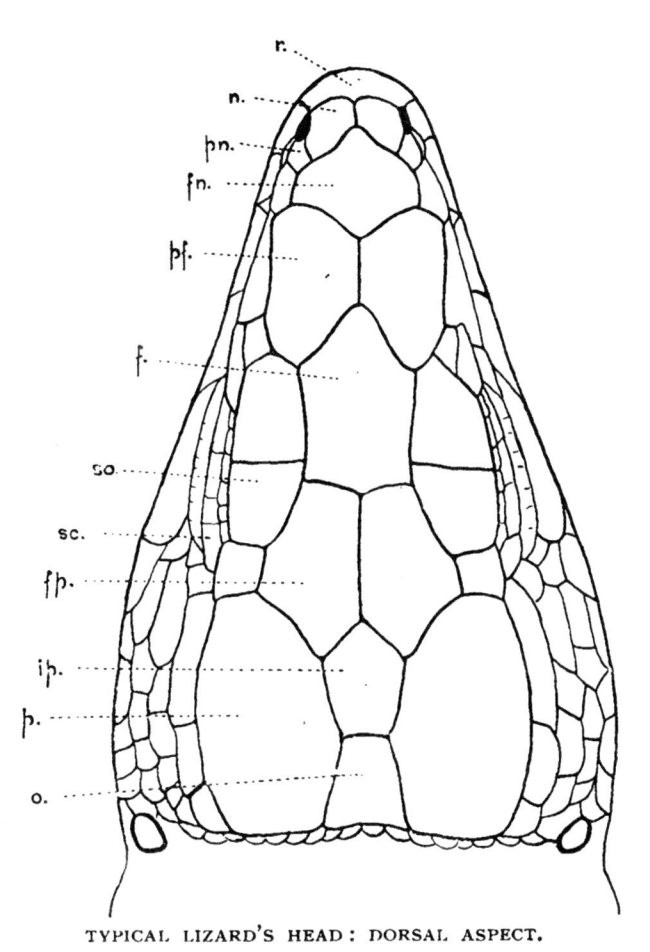

[*Facing p.* 86.

Lastly, from this aspect, some smaller shields will be found towards the front end of the snout. If any separate the nasal shields from each other they are called the inter-nasal, and those just behind the nasals may be described as fronto-nasal (FN.) since they are placed in the region between the frontal and nasal shields. The single shield at the very front of the snout is called the rostral (R.) or beak shield; it is more prominent from above in some species than in others.

This completes the terminology of the shields of the vertex, and though the names at first sight appear somewhat formidable, they are so descriptive that a careful study of the arrangement as shown in the diagram will make the matter quite clear. It remains to describe the shields on the other two surfaces of the head in a similar manner.

2. *The Lateral Aspect.*

The shields or scales at the side of the head are those which are in relation to the nostrils, the eyes, and the line of division between the upper and lower halves of the mouth when closed, the labial region.

The names of the shields or scales which must be noted on this aspect are as follows:—

(*a*) The nasal; (*b*) the superior labials; (*c*) the inferior labials; (*d*) the supra-ciliary; (*e*) the loreal; (*f*) the pre-loreal; (*g*) the infra-labials; (*h*) the rostral.

We have already defined the rostral (R.); it is seen again from this lateral view of the head, and the same applies to the nasals (N.), which are at once recognised by the opening of the nostril through them.

The superior labials (L.) are the scales which take the place of the upper lip in snakes and lizards. Their number varies greatly even in the same species, and very often is different on the two sides of the head of the same specimen. Thus it is very common in the adder to find eight upper labials on the right side, and seven or nine on the left side. They are often termed simply lip scales. Seven are represented in the diagram, the three largest being those beneath and posterior to the eye.

Immediately above the eye will be noticed a row of much smaller scales, which are named, from their position, the supra-ciliary scales (SC.). In front of the eye are two scales of irregular shape, the loreals (LO. and LO'.), posterior and anterior. The word "loreal" is derived from the Latin *lorum*, a thong or strap, the term being originally applied to a corslet of leathern thongs, which had a somewhat scaly appearance. Hence the term "lore" in ornithology, to define the space between the bill and the eye which in some birds is bare and devoid of feathers, hence scaly-looking. The word has the same significance in the lizards, and refers to the position of the scale between the eye and the snout. A further development is from the Latin *lorica*, a coat of mail, hence the order of reptiles, the Loricata,

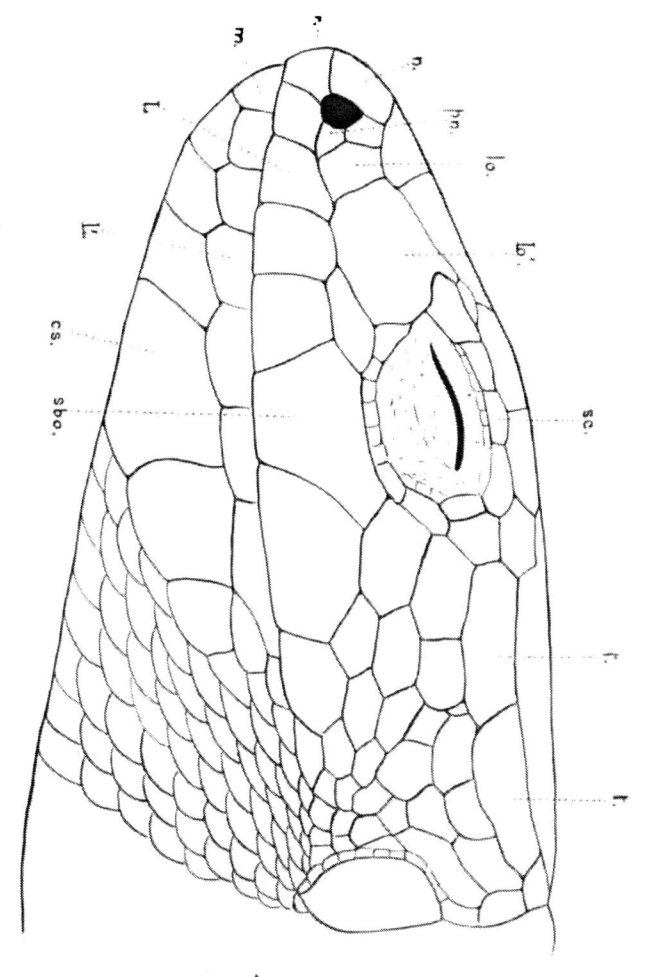

TYPICAL LIZARD'S HEAD: LATERAL ASPECT.

[Facing p. 88.

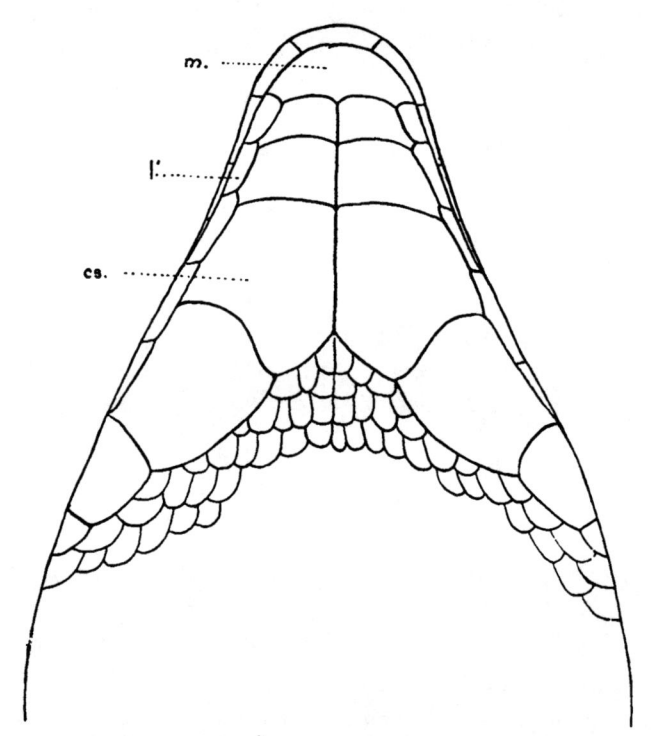

TYPICAL LIZARD'S HEAD: VENTRAL ASPECT.

[Facing p. 89.

SPECIFIC CHARACTERS OF BRITISH LIZARDS

including the crocodiles, which are characterised by the plate armour with which their bodies are protected.

The only other scales claiming attention on the side of the head are those in the position of the lower lip of other animals, namely, the *inferior labials*, or lower lip scales (L'.); and immediately below these the chin shields, the tops of which are seen, the rest of these scales belonging to the under surface. Like the upper labials the lower ones vary considerably, and should always be examined.

3. THE VENTRAL ASPECT.

We now come to the third and last aspect of the head, that which is out of sight until the specimen is held up or turned on its back. The scaling here is very simple. There are first the lower labials, which were seen partly from the side. The only others which need concern us here are the scales of the chin region. The most anterior of these which extends between the two rows of lower labials is termed the *mental* shield, or chin shield proper. Those just behind the mental are, as we should expect, the *post-mental* shields, and these merge into the scales of the throat farther back.

The rest of the scales covering the body present no difficulty. They take their names from their position, *dorsal* on the back, *ventral* on the belly, *caudal* and *sub-caudal* on or under the tail, *anal* or *pre-anal* in front of the anal aperture.

The reader who has mastered the few preceding pages will have no trouble in understanding the descriptions of the specific characters of the lizards, though these would otherwise be unintelligible. He will now be able to appreciate the statement that normally in *Lacerta vivipara* there is a single post-nasal shield, and a single anterior loreal shield, while in *L. agilis* there is usually a single post-nasal and two superimposed anterior loreals, the three shields forming a triangle.

We are now in a position to enumerate the specific characters of the British lizards, as they are given in the British Museum *Catalogue of Reptiles* (second edition, vol. ii. 1885, and vol. iii. 1887, by G. A. Boulenger, F.R.S.).

"Family ANGUIDÆ. Genus *Anguis*.

"No lateral fold. Scales roundish, arranged quincuncially on the back, forming vertical series on the sides. No limbs. Teeth fanglike. Palate toothless.

"Europe, Western Asia, Algeria.

"*Anguis fragilis*, the Slow-worm.

"Frontal large, its anterior angle wedged in between a pair of pre-frontals; an azygos pre-frontal in front of the latter, separated from the nasal by two small shields; 1 or 2 small azygos shields behind the very small rostral; nasal very small, separated from the latter by one shield; labials and loreals small,

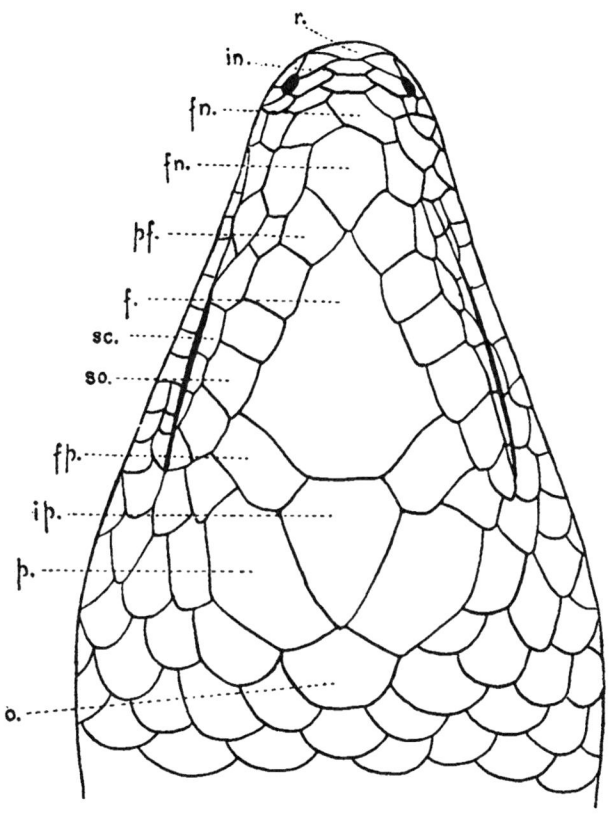

HEAD OF INDIAN SLOW-WORM.
OPHISAURUS GRACILIS.

[*Facing p.* 90.

numerous; inter-parietal as long as and broader than the parietals and in contact with a small occipital; a small fronto-parietal between the supra-oculars and the inter-parietal, and a larger shield between the supra-oculars and the parietal; supra-oculars 5 or 6. Ear-opening minute, usually hidden. Scales smooth, median dorsal and ventrals broad, hexagonal; 24 to 28 scales round the middle of the body. Tail at least as long as the body. Young silvery above, with a black vertebral line; sides and lower surfaces blackish. In the adult these markings often disappear, or may be replaced by a series of dark dots, and the colour of the upper surfaces becomes brown or bronzy. A variety (*colchica*), in which the ear-opening appears to be normally distinct, is distinguished by having scattered pale blue spots on the back.

"From snout to vent, 195 mm.; tail, 230.

"Family LACERTIDÆ. Genus *Lacerta*.

"Head shields normal. Nostril pierced between two or three nasals, bordered by the first upper labial, or separated from that shield by a very narrow rim. Lower eyelid scaly, or with a small transparent disc. Collar well marked. Dorsal scales much smaller than caudals, not or but feebly imbricate; ventral shields tetragonal, feebly imbricate, smooth. Digits subcylindrical or compressed, with smooth, tubercular, or indistinctly keeled lamellæ inferiorly. Femoral pores. Tail long, cylindrical.

"Europe; Northern and Western Asia; Africa, north of the equator."

"*Lacerta vivipara*, the Common Lizard.

"Head small; snout moderate, obtuse. Rostral not touching the nostril; normally a single post-nasal, a single anterior loreal, in contact with the fronto-nasal, and 4 upper labials anterior to the sub-ocular; no granules between the supra-oculars and the supra-ciliaries, occipital small, usually smaller than the inter-parietal; temple covered with irregular flat scales, among which a masseteric is often, and a tympanic constantly, distinct. Gular fold feebly marked, or absent. 14 to 21 gular scales on a line between the collar and the third pair of chin shields; collar with serrated edge, composed of 7 or 9 plates. Dorsal scales hexagonal, longer than broad, more or less distinctly keeled, not or but slightly imbricate, somewhat smaller than the laterals, which are smooth; nuchal scales roundish, smooth, or nearly so; 2 lateral scales correspond to the length of a ventral plate; 26 to 37 scales across the middle of the body. Ventral plates in 6 or 8 longitudinal series, the second series on each side from the median ventral line the largest; 24 to 30 transverse series. Two semicircles of scales border the pre-anal shield. The adpressed limbs meet, or the hind-limb reaches the wrist or the elbow. Foot usually longer than the head. Femoral pores, 7 to 13. Tail thick, once

COMMON LIZARD.

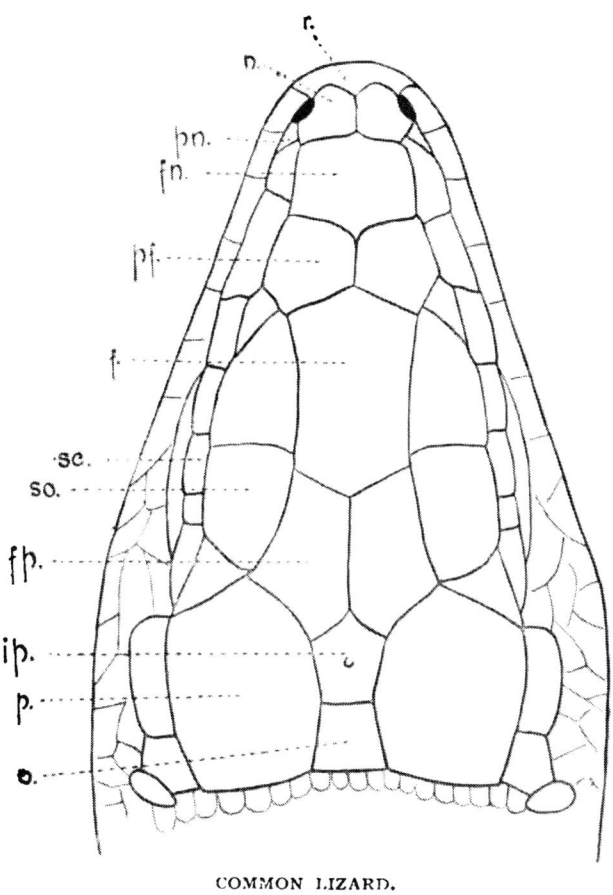

[Facing p. 91.

SAND LIZARD.

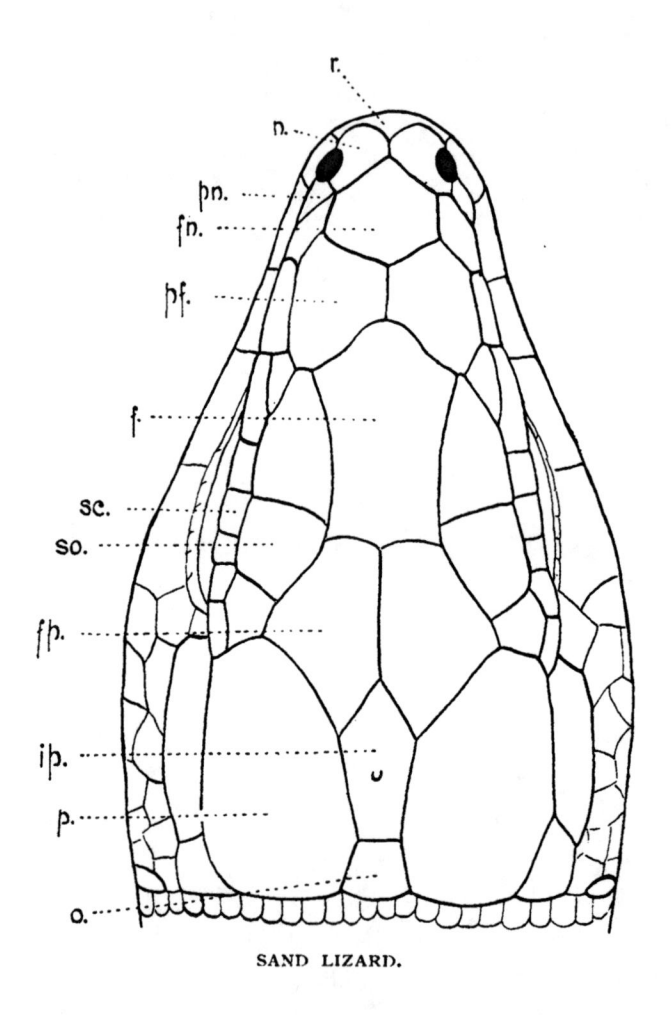

[Facing p. 93.

and two-fifths to once and two-thirds as long as head and body; caudal scales large, upper strongly keeled and pointed posteriorly. Brown, yellowish, or reddish above in the adult, with small darker and lighter spots; frequently a blackish vertebral streak and a dark lateral band edged with yellowish; lower surfaces orange or vermilion in the male, largely spotted with black; yellow or pale orange in the female, immaculate or scantily spotted with black. Newly-born young almost black, which colouration sometimes persists in the adult.

	Male.	Female.
	Mm.	Mm.
Total length	151	178
Head	12	12
Width of head	9	9
From end of snout to fore-limb	19	23
From end of snout to vent	53	73
Fore-limb	17	18
Hind-limb	24	25
Tail	98	105

" Northern and Central Europe; Northern Asia.

"*Lacerta agilis*, the Sand Lizard.

"Habit stouter, snout shorter than in *L. viridis*. Rostral not touching the nostril; 1 or 2 postnasals; frequently 2 superimposed anterior loreals; normally 4 upper labials anterior to the subocular—no granules between the supra-oculars and the supra-ciliaries; occipital small, shorter and usually narrower than the inter-parietal; temples covered with flat scales; 2 or 3 large temporals in contact with the parietal; no tympanic. Gular fold feebly marked, or absent. 14 to 22 gular scales on a line between the collar and the third pair of chin shields; collar with serrated edge, composed of 7 to 11 plates. Dorsal scales hexagonal, strongly keeled, larger on the sides, where they are feebly keeled or smooth; 2 or 3 lateral scales correspond to the length of a ventral plate; 34 to 52 scales across the middle of the body. Ventral plates in 6 or 8 longitudinal series, the second series on each side from the median ventral line the largest; 25 to 32 transverse series. The hind-limb never reaches beyond the elbow of the adpressed fore-limb. Foot not, or but very slightly, longer than the head. Femoral pores, 10 to 18. Tail once and a half to once and two-thirds the length of head and body; upper caudal scales strongly keeled, pointed posteriorly.

"Northern and Central Europe; Western Asia.

"(a) FORMA TYPICA.

"Usually a single post-nasal and two superposed anterior loreals, the three shields forming a triangle. Median dorsal scales very narrow, sharply differentiated from the broader laterals; 34 to 46 scales across the middle of the body. Usually a single semicircle of scales bordering the anal, none of which are much enlarged. Young greyish brown above with longi-

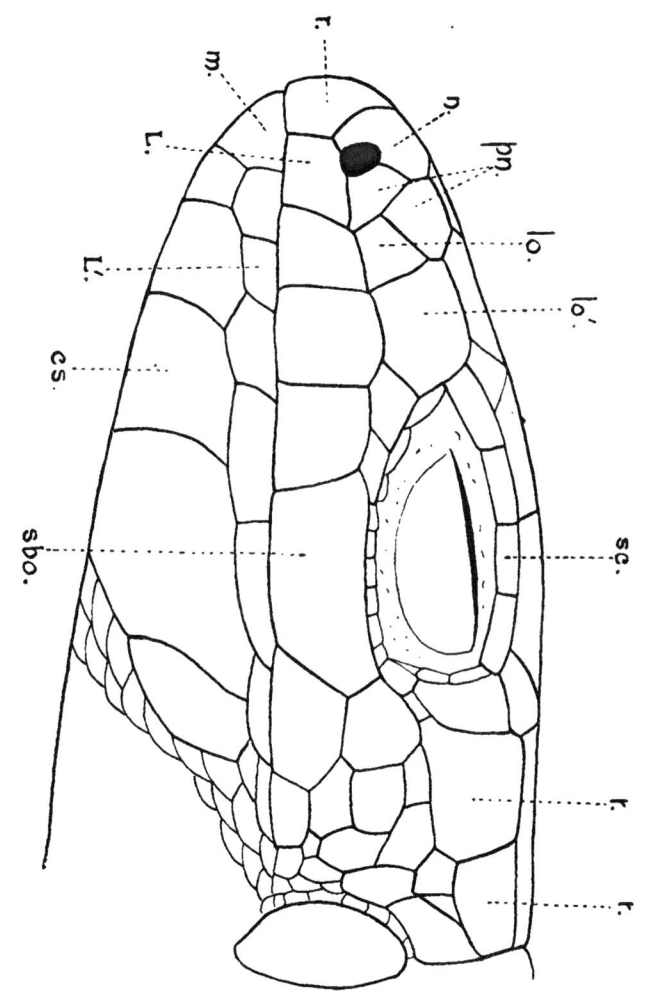

SAND LIZARD: LATERAL ASPECT.

[*Facing p.* 94.

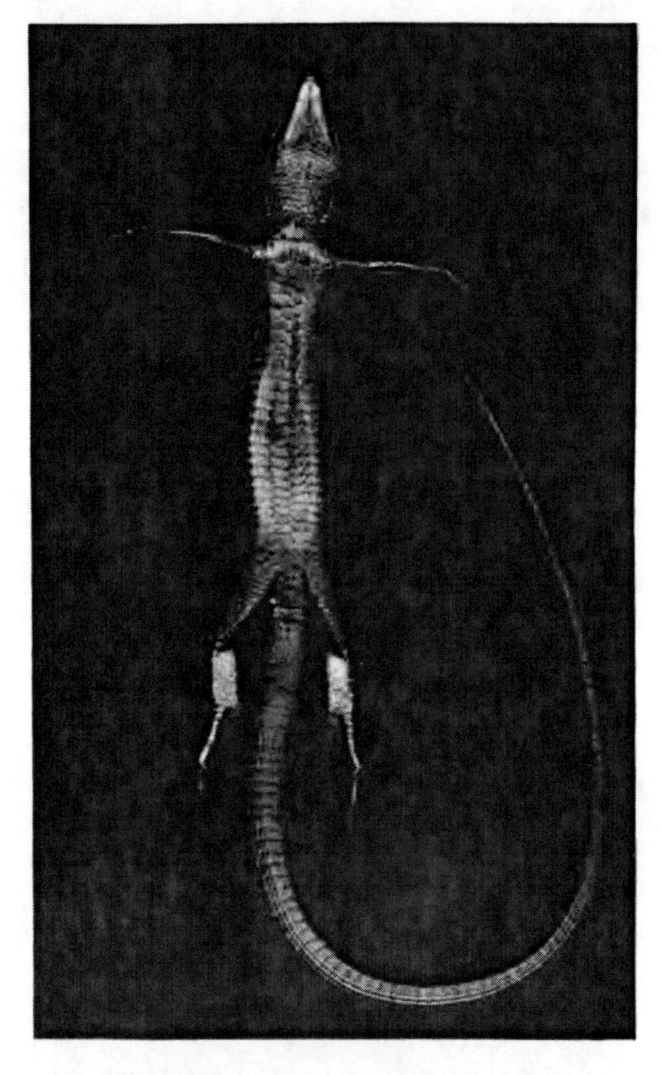

GREEN LIZARD: SCALING OF VENTRAL SURFACE.

[*Facing p.* 55.

tudinal series of white, black-edged ocelli; no light vertebral streak, lower surfaces whitish, immaculate. Adult female, brown or greyish above, the vertebral zone darker than the sides of the back, with large dark brown spots with a central white shaft or round spot; usually the larger spots form 3 longitudinal series on the body; belly cream-coloured, with or without black spots. Male, during the breeding season, green on the sides and lower surfaces, rarely also on the back; sides black-dotted, usually with lighter ocelli; lower surfaces more or less abundantly spotted with black. A form is distinguished by the unspotted reddish-brown or brick-red back (*L. rubra*).

	Male.	Female.
	Mm.	Mm.
Total length	206	212
Head	20	18
Width of head . . .	14	12
From end of snout to fore-limb	29	27
From end of snout to vent . .	78	87
Fore-limb	21	25
Hind-limb	31	34
Tail	128	125

"South of England; Northern, Central, and Eastern France; Belgium; Holland; Switzerland; Germany; Austria; Denmark; Sweden; Russia.

"*Lacerta viridis*, the Green Lizard.

"Head moderate; snout moderately long, obtuse. Rostral usually touching or entering the nostril;

normally 2 regularly superposed post-nasals and 4 upper labials anterior to the sub-ocular; a series of granules may be present between the supra-oculars and the supra-ciliaries; occipital narrower than the frontal; temples covered with flat scales; 2 large temporal shields in contact with the parietal. Gular fold usually distinct; 16 to 25 gular scales on a line between the collar and the third pair of chin shields; collar with serrated edge, composed of 7 to 12 plates. Dorsal scales oval-hexagonal or rhomboidal, keeled, not or but slightly larger on the sides, where 2 or 3 correspond to the length of a ventral plate; 40 to 58 scales across the middle of the body. Ventral plates in 6 or 8 longitudinal series, the second series of each side from the median ventral line the largest; 25 to 31 transverse series. Pre-anal plate bordered by two semicircles of small plates. The hind-limb reaches between the wrist of the adpressed fore-limb and the shoulder. Foot, in the female and young, longer than the head. Femoral pores, 12 to 20. Tail usually about twice as long as head and body; caudal scales keeled, pointed posteriorly.

"Central and Southern Europe; South-western Asia.

"(a) FORMA TYPICA.

"Granules between the supra-oculars and the supra-ciliaries often absent; occipital usually very small; usually a distinct masseteric plate but no tympanic.

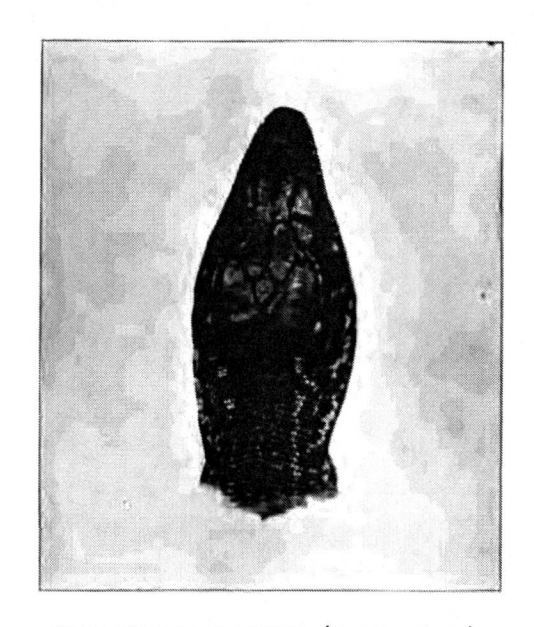

HEAD OF GREEN LIZARD (FROM ABOVE).

[*Facing p.* 97.

42 to 50 scales across the middle of the body, the laterals a little larger than the median dorsals. Usually only 6 longitudinal rows of ventrals. Femoral pores, 13 to 18. Young, brown or green above, with one or two more or less distinct yellowish lateral streaks, which may persist in the adult female. Adult, green above, uniform or dotted, or spotted with black, or blackish olive speckled with green, lower surfaces yellow, uniform; throat usually blue, especially in the males.

	Male.	Female.
	Mm.	Mm.
Total length	400	355
Head	28	24
Width of head	18	15
From end of snout to fore-limb	43	42
From end of snout to vent . .	110	120
Fore-limb	36	39
Hind-limb	64	64
Tail	290	235

"Italy, France, Switzerland, Austria, Germany, Russia, Channel Islands.

"*Lacerta muralis*, the Wall Lizard.

"Head rather long, more or less depressed. Rostral not entering the nostril, normally a single post-nasal and 4 upper labials anterior to the sub-ocular (often 5 anterior labials in vars. *hispanica* and *bedriagæ*); a series of granules between the supra-oculars and the supra-ciliaries; occipital small or moderate; temple granular, usually with distinct masseteric and tympanic plates. Gular fold more or less distinct; 20 to 35 gular scales on a line between the collar and the third pair of chin shields; collar even-edged or, rarely, slightly serrated, composed of 9 to 11 plates. Dorsal scales granular, smooth or feebly keeled, laterals as large or a little smaller; 40 to 80 scales across the middle of the body; 3 to 5 lateral scales correspond to the length of a ventral plate. Ventrals squarish, broader than long, in 6, rarely 8, longitudinal, and 25 to 32 transverse series. Pre-anal bordered by one or two semicircles of small scales. Limbs rather elongate, especially in the males, in which the hind-limb reaches the shoulder or beyond. Scales on upper surface of tibia smaller than dorsals. Femoral pores, 13 to 29. Tail usually about twice as long as head and body; caudal scales more or less distinctly keeled, with truncate or very obtusely pointed posterior border.

"Central and Southern Europe, North-west Africa, Asia Minor, Northern Persia, Syria.

"(a) FORMA TYPICA.

"Size comparatively small. Head usually rather strongly depressed. The hind-limb rarely reaches the axilla in the female. 40 to 65 scales across the middle of the body; 3 or 4 lateral scales correspond to the length of a ventral. Upper parts brown or greyish, variously spotted, marbled, or streaked

WALL LIZARD.

with blackish; lower surfaces white, yellow, pink, or red, uniform or (in males) more or less largely spotted with black; outer ventrals frequently blue.

	Male.	Female.
	Mm.	Mm.
Total length	187	180
Head	16	13
Width of head	11	9
From end of snout to fore-limb	25	22
From end of snout to vent	62	62
Fore-limb	23	20
Hind-limb	35	30
Tail	125	118

"Central and Southern Europe; North-western Africa; Asia Minor to Northern Persia."

The above is the technical account of the specific characters of the British species of lizards, and with the explanation we have given of the terms used, any member of a field club will be able to trace these characters out for himself on a specimen. It is hoped that one result will be that a few field naturalists here and there will take up the subject of the variations in size, colour, and proportions, of the lizards of the locality, and thus add to our present knowledge of the question. We would urge those who do look into the matter to keep most careful records of every specimen examined, to have them incorporated in their Society's *Transactions*, and to send any specimens presenting marked abnormalities to the British Museum of Natural History, at South

Kensington. The same injunction may be taken as applying to our snakes. As a mere matter of mental training and education, it is of infinitely more value to master accurately the details of such a subject, than to acquire a superficial smattering of half a dozen sciences. The following explains the lettering of the diagrams:—

C.S. Chin shields.
f. Frontal.
fn. Fronto-nasal.
fp. Fronto-parietal.
in. Inter-nasal.
ip. Inter-parietal.
L. Upper labial.
L'. Lower labial.
r. Rostral.
sc. Supra-ciliary.

Lo. Anterior loreal.
Lo'. Posterior loreal.
m. Mental.
n. Nasal.
o. Occipital.
p. Parietal.
pn. Post-nasal.
pf. Præ-frontal.
Sbo. Sub-ocular.
so. Supra-orbital.
t. Temporal.

[TABLE.]

CLASSIFICATION OF BRITISH LIZARDS.

Order.	Suborder.	Family.	Genus.	Species.	Common Name.
SQUAMATA.	LACERTILIA.	LACERTIDÆ.	*Lacerta*	*vivipara.*	Common Lizard.
			Lacerta	*agilis.*	Sand Lizard.
		ANGUIDÆ.	*Anguis*	*fragilis.*	Slow-worm.
	LACERTILIA.	LACERTIDÆ.	*Lacerta*	*viridis.*	Green Lizard.
	,,	,,	,,	*muralis.*	Wall Lizard.

(Channel Islands: Green Lizard, Wall Lizard.)

CHAPTER XI

THE FRAGILITY OF THE TAIL IN LIZARDS

IT is a matter of very common knowledge and observation that in some families and species of lizards, the tail is extremely fragile. The European slow-worm (*Anguis fragilis*) takes its specific name from this circumstance. This anomalous reptile if startled or taken hold of at once stiffens its tail into a rigid condition, and very slight violence is then sufficient to cause a fracture of the tail, either complete or partial. If complete, the portion of tail broken off remains in the grasp while the lizard escapes; if partial, the fracture appears on the ventral aspect of the tail as a transverse crack, but remains attached along the dorsal aspect. When the lizard thus makes the tail rigid, a very slight blow is enough to cause part of the tail to come away, and the reptile is apparently none the worse for the loss of a portion of its anatomy.

Ophiologists have accounted for this remarkable phenomenon by the peculiarity of structure exhibited by some families of Lacertilia in the caudal vertebræ. Thus Professor Cope in his monumental work on *The*

Crocodiles, Lizards, and Snakes of North America, says (p. 190): "In a good many families the caudal vertebræ are divided by a transverse fissure or suture in front of the middle, which often splits the base and sometimes the length of the diapophysis. Such a structure is seen in Iguanidæ (*Iguana, Sauromalus, Sceloporus, Dipsosaurus*), Anolidæ, Anguidæ (*Celestus*), Teiidæ (*Tupinambis, Cnemidophorus*), Lacertidæ (*Lacerta*), and Scincidæ (*Gongylus, Eumeces*). In *Dipsosaurus, Anolis*, and *Lacerta*, the neural spines of the vertebræ (caudal) are double; in the other genera named, single. In *Varanidæ, Helodermidæ, Gerronotus, Crotaphytus*, and *Phrynosoma*, the caudal centra are undivided, and the neural spines are single. In *Ophisaurus* the centra are undivided, and the neural spines double. The centra are excessively thin in *Ophisaurus*, so that they break more readily than they disarticulate."

In *Sceloporus*, which is a common species in Mexico and the Southern United States, this segmentation of the centra of the caudal vertebræ is present only from about the eighth vertebræ. Professor Packard in his *Text-Book of Zoology* (p. 502), says: "In many lizards (*Lacerta, Iguana*, and the *Geckos*), the middle of each caudal vertebra has a thin cartilaginous partition, and it is at this point that the tails of these lizards break off so easily when seized."

In British text-books on Zoology, the anatomy of the Reptilia is usually very deficiently dealt with; but Dr. Hans Gadow's recently published work on

Amphibia and Reptiles goes into some detail on the point. He says (p. 495): "The caudal vertebræ of the *Geckones* and of most *Lacertæ* are liable to break across, like those of *Sphenodon*. They are enabled to do this owing to a transverse split, which makes its appearance with the ossification of the vertebral bodies and extends later into and across the neural arch and the various lateral processes. This split is ultimately referable to a transverse septum of cartilage, wrongly called chordal cartilage, which develops in the shell of the body of the vertebra, destroys the chorda, and extends peripherally. The cells of this septum retain throughout life their juvenile quasi-embryonic character. When the tail is broken off—and this always happens at such a septum—the cells of the remaining half reproduce a new tail." Again, Dr. Gadow, on p. 503 of the same work, says: "Each vertebral centrum consists of a cartilaginous tube, more or less calcified or ossified, with a narrow waist and a cartilaginous septum in the middle. In the tail this septum, which is only slightly invaded by ossification, coincides exactly with the line of transverse division of the vertebræ into an anterior and a posterior half. This is the level where the tail breaks off and whence it is renewed."

We may therefore say that the accepted explanation of the phenomenon of the fragility of the tail in some lizards, is that it is due to a peculiar condition of the vertebræ, namely, the development of a cartilaginous septum in the middle of the caudal vertebral centra, whereby these vertebræ are enabled to fracture transversely at the position of the septum. The object of this chapter is to inquire into the truth or otherwise of this view, and to point out how this explanation is insufficient to account for *all* the facts. Further, if possible, to show that other factors play a part in the process, without which it could not occur.

THEORETICAL CONSIDERATIONS.

It had long appeared to me that the views enunciated above, and copied into all text-books, even if true as far as they went, afforded but a partial explanation of the possibility of a lizard to lose a portion of its tail with ease. The mere fact that an animal has sustained a transverse fracture of a bone in a limb or organ, is *not enough* to account for that limb becoming detached from the body.

Bones are not the only parts of an organ, they are kept in position by ligaments and by muscles acting upon them, by connective tissue affording further support, and finally by the integument enclosing more or less firmly the whole organ or limb. (An appendage, such as the tail of a lizard, is practically an axial limb.) The usual arrangement of these tissues other than bones has the effect, when a fracture occurs, of keeping the limb in connection with the body until a more or less perfect union has taken place at the point of fracture. In other words, for a limb to become detached from the body, requires a division of the soft parts surrounding it, as well as a fracture of the bone. It therefore may be concluded, theoretically, that the dropping of the lizard's tail must depend upon the peculiar arrangement of the muscles and integument quite as much, if not more than, upon the ease with which the vertebræ are enabled to break across.

The first problem which presents itself in this connection is this. Seeing that in most animals possessed of long tails the muscles are attached from one vertebra to another, allowing of a certain amount of intervertebral movement, but keeping the tail, as a whole, attached to the body even if a fracture of a vertebra occurs, what special muscular arrangement exists in those lizards which drop their tails when this accident happens? Secondly, even if by some anatomical arrangement the muscles do not keep the tail attached to the body, how is it that the skin or integument always breaks all round the circumference of the tail exactly over the point of the fractured vertebræ?

(The species of lizards first used to investigate these points were *Anguis fragilis*, the slow-worm, and *Lacerta viridis*, the green lizard, of the Continent and Channel Islands.)

1. *Anguis fragilis*, the Slow-worm.

Selecting a specimen from my collection, I proceeded to carefully break off a portion of the tail. It was

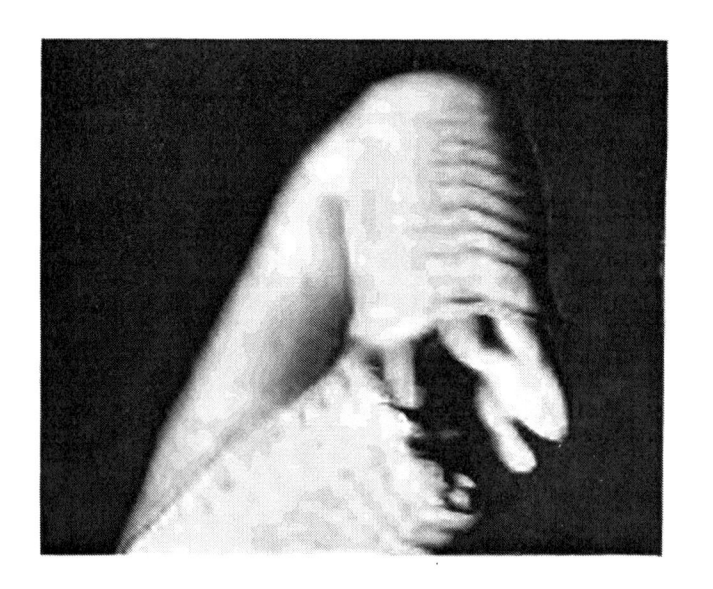

SLOW-WORM: ALMOST COMPLETE FRACTURE.

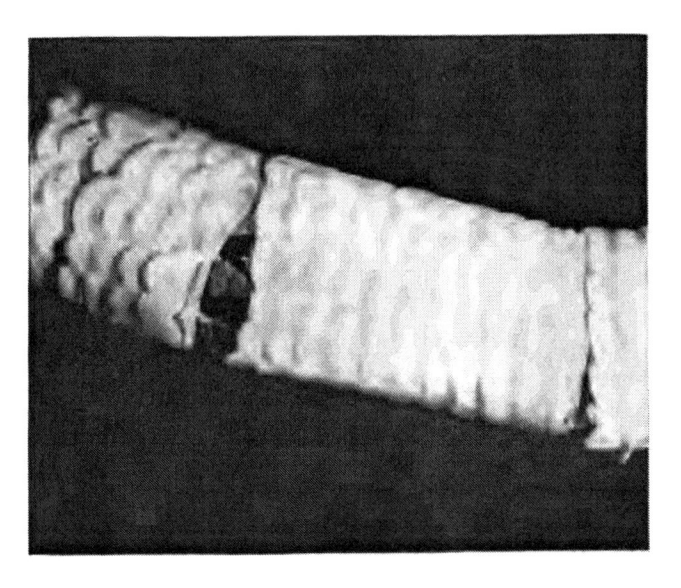

PORTION OF TAIL OF SLOW-WORM: TWO INCOMPLETE

at once evident that while the integument ruptured readily round the circumference of the lower half (the ventral half) of the tail at the point of fracture, it did not do so nearly so easily on the dorsal aspect. In fact, some degree of force was necessary to complete the division of the skin all round. But by bending the two halves of the tail, as one would bend a stick across the knees, the fracture was completed. The structures thus separated in the following order:—

    First, the ventral integument;
    Then the ventral muscles;
    Then the lateral integument and muscles on each side;
    Then the dorsal muscles;
    Lastly, the dorsal integument.

This indicates the degree of ease with which the parts separated, the ventral aspect rupturing most easily, the dorsal remaining intact the longest. The first thing that struck me was that the initial point of separation was in the skin, not, apparently, in the vertebra, and one naturally wondered whether this corresponded to the position of the cartilaginous septum. The next thing that compelled notice was that the two separated ends of the tail—the proximal and the distal ends—presented a marked contrast. The proximal end, still of course attached to the body, exhibited eight muscles which had been separated from their attachments to the distal portion, giving the proximal end a stellate appearance; while the distal end exhibited a plain, smooth surface, no muscles being visible. Closer inspection at once revealed the spaces into which these eight muscles fitted, seen as holes dipping into the distal portion of the tail. The appearance of the two ends is seen in the accompanying illustration.

Taking next the portion of the tail which had come away from the body, I refractured this in several places, with precisely the same results. In each fracture the proximal portion retained the eight muscles, while in each distal portion the positions into which these muscles fitted were seen as holes. The shape of each of these muscles was roughly triangular, thick at the proximal attached end, tapering to a point at the distal separable end. In doing this, I found that the fracture always took place at the *same point as regards the muscles*, nowhere else. I next dissected one of the fractured pieces of the tail. The integument is extremely tough, and difficult to cut in the slow-worm. To the naked eye, as one dissects it, this skin appears to be disposed in two layers,—an external thick layer covered by scales, and an internal thin layer. The external thick layer strips off all round the tail, leaving the thin internal layer, which is an investing membrane for the tail. It is whitish in colour, and tough to dissect. An incision was made along the whole length of this internal layer of tissue, in the median dorsal line. This was carefully reflected laterally, with the result that the eight muscles came

INTEGUMENT DISSECTED OFF A
FRACTURED TAIL.

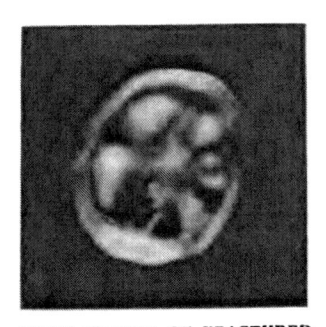

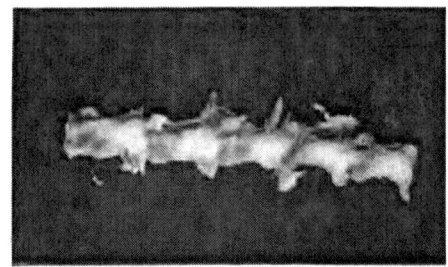

FIVE VERTEBRÆ FROM TAIL OF SLOW-WORM.

PROXIMAL END OF FRACTURED TAIL.

CROSS-SECTION OF FRACTURED
TAIL.

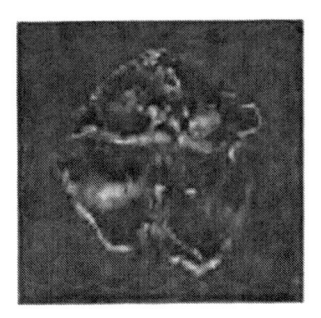

DISTAL END OF FRACTURED TAIL.

off with it, leaving the caudal vertebræ lying free in the dissection. The appearance of the integument with the muscles attached is seen in illustration, which gives a better idea of it than any description. Turning next to the condition of the vertebræ, it was with the greatest interest that I found them to be intact. The separation had taken place at the intervertebral articulation at both ends of the fractured piece of tail, and not in the centre of the bodies of the vertebræ as supposed. I photographed this portion of the caudal vertebral column, and it is here reproduced.

So that, in this case at any rate, when the tail was broken off, the fracture did not take place at the cartilaginous septum, as is said always to happen.

Looking closely at the arrangement of the muscles, it was easily seen that their arrangement was curiously adapted to permit of their readily separating. This arrangement is best described perhaps by the term "dove-tailed." They fit into each other just as the handle of a cricket bat is dovetailed into the blade. And, further, they separate from each other just in the same way that the handle of a bat is forced apart from the blade, so that when in process of separation they look like the fingers of one's two hands interdigitating.

These eight muscles are not equal in size, nor are they disposed at equal intervals round the vertebral column. Six of them are longer than the other two, the two short ones, which are the thickest, being ventral. Diagrammatically, the positions of the eight muscles may be thus represented—

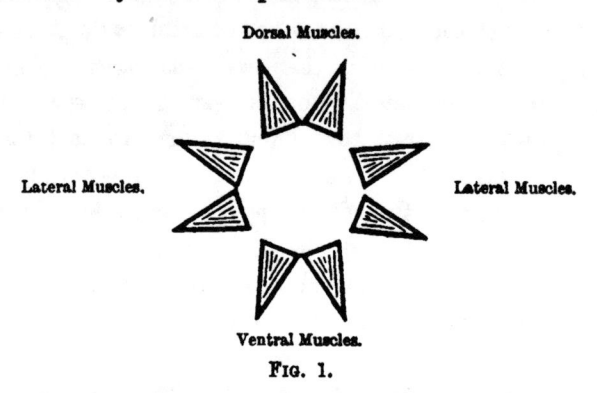

Dorsal Muscles.

Lateral Muscles.   Lateral Muscles.

Ventral Muscles.
Fig. 1.

The two dorsal muscles are separated from each other by a somewhat wider interval than any of the others, so that they are, strictly speaking, dorso-lateral, the dorsal median line being free from muscle.

The relative shortness of the two ventral muscles accounts for the fact that the fracture begins on the ventral side and is easiest here.

The thick end or attached end of these muscles is very firmly inserted into the inner layer of the integument. The thin tapering end lies practically free in the sheaths provided for its reception. After all, this is the only arrangement which would permit of that easy fragility of the tail under consideration. It is impossible to fracture the tail opposite the points of origin of these muscles in the integument; any attempt to do so results in their separation where the ends taper to the free point in the spaces made by the fibrous septa in which they lie.

2. *Lacerta viridis*, the Green Lizard.

These anatomical arrangements on which this phenomenon depends are even better seen in the green lizard, where the scaling of the tail adds another factor not so easily made out in the slow-worm. The scales in the latter are extremely small, in the green

Fracture.
No fracture.
Fracture.
No fracture.
Fracture.
No fracture.
Fracture, and so on.

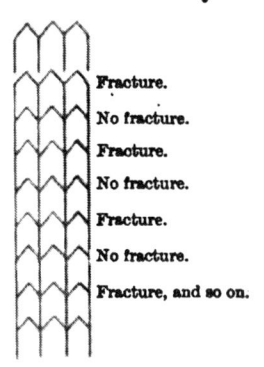

FIG. 2.

lizard they are large and elongated. When I proceeded to confirm the results above described, by fracturing the tail in green lizards, it was found that these caudal scales have a definite position with regard to the muscles. One naturally expected that the fracture took place between two rows of scales, not across a row, but I was not prepared to find that it occurred at definite intervals of scales, and only at those intervals. But, of course, it simply is that a certain number of scales correspond to each muscle-length, and that number, as a matter of fact, is two. The length of two scales is the length of one muscle, so that the fracture is found to occur at intervals of two scales. One cannot make the tail fracture at the end of the scale next to that which covered the termination of a previous fracture. The diagram on p. 111 may explain this more clearly.

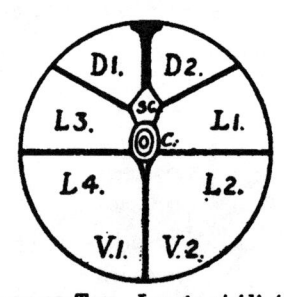

FIG. 3.—SECTION OF TAIL, *Lacerta viridis* (diagrammatic).
SC is spinal cord. C is centrum of vertebra.
D 1, D 2, are positions of the two dorsal muscles.
V 1, V 2, „ „ „ ventral muscles.
L 1, 2, 3, 4, „ „ four lateral muscles.
Note.—There are three partitions on each side, the ventral one on each side holds *two* muscles, a ventral and a lateral muscle.

There is thus a very well-marked metameric segmentation in the tail of these lizards, each segment being marked externally by the interval between every second scale, though no differentiation is apparent. Just as in the case of the slow-worm, so in the green lizard, if the skin be dissected off a part that is fractured, the muscles come off with it, and present the same arrangement seen before. The caudal ver-

FRAGILITY OF THE TAIL IN LIZARDS

tebræ are left intact, or may be so left, and there is seen a number of fibrous septa running from the vertebral processes to the integument, thus dividing the tail into compartments into which the muscles are fitted, and out of which the thin tapering ends readily escape when the fracture occurs. The diagram on the opposite page shows the arrangement of these septa.

These septa are not continuous longitudinally, but each is inserted into the integument of its own segment, opposite the end of the scales of that segment, so that here the fracture takes place. Here again, as in the slow-worm, the proximal end of the fragment of tail shows the eight muscles protruding, while the distal end shows the intervertebral articulation surface intact, the fracture having occurred *between two vertebræ*, not across one. On illustration facing page 108 these two ends are seen photographed from the fresh dissection. Both these fractures show the articulating surfaces of the vertebræ intact. In a word, there is no fracture of the caudal vertebræ in these cases, but a simple disarticulation or dislocation.

It was thus concluded that fracture of the tail in the green lizard, as in the slow-worm, depends mainly upon the peculiar arrangement of muscles and integument; that this fracture takes place or may do at definite intervals corresponding to the end of every second caudal scale; and that this position as regards the caudal vertebræ was at an intervertebral articulation. Given a fracture at any point, one may say with certainty where any other fracture may occur, by simply counting the scales; the other fractures will be only at the ends of the rows of scales numbering 2, 4, 6, 8, 10, and so on, from the first fractured point. It should be added that the explanation here offered to account for the fragility of the tail is not an accepted view, but it is one which any observant field naturalist can examine for himself on the first slow-worm he encounters.

It is quite obvious that no special arrangement of ossification in the vertebræ would be sufficient to account for the phenomenon, unless some highly specialised form of muscular and scale structure also existed. Lack of ossification in a bone may be a cause of fracture; it will not account for a limb or an appendage dropping off from the body, as do the tails of some lizards.

CHAPTER XII

COLOUR VARIATION IN LIZARDS

THE PROBLEM—FACTORS CONCERNED—EVIDENCE OF SEX INFLUENCE—EVIDENCE OF AGE INFLUENCE—CONCLUSION—REFERENCES.

From what has been said in the foregoing pages under the headings of the various species of British lizards, it will be quite evident to the reader that there is a very marked degree of colour variation to be found in these reptiles. In that respect they resemble the snakes, in which the same phenomenon is equally pronounced. The present writer has on various previous occasions dealt with the problem as presented in the order of serpents, and a reference to the literature in that group is appended at the end of this chapter. It remains, therefore, to review the principles applicable to the subject with special reference to the lizards, and to endeavour to ascertain to what extent the processes of colour variation in lizards are due to the same or similar causes as those proved to be responsible for the colour variation of serpents.

"To state the problem clearly, it is necessary at the outset to recognise the distinction between *protective colouration* and *colour variation*. The former term is used to describe the resemblance in appearance between many creatures and their surroundings, by means of which resemblance the members of the species are protected from attack, and thus the species from extinction. Thus every sportsman knows how difficult it is at a little distance to distinguish partridges from the earth on which they are crouching. . . . But this protective colouration is quite a different phenomenon from that of colour variation. This latter term is descriptive of the varying colours seen in any given species, whether that species exhibits any protective colouring or not."[1]

In the present case, in other words, the problem is not to account for the specific markings and colourings of the different lizards which may be protective or not, but to ascertain the reason why these specific markings and colours exhibit such striking variations, *i.e.* to solve the problem of colour variation in lizards.

Every student of natural history knows that there are many factors which are usually considered to take part in producing colour variation in animals. Most of these factors, perhaps, will fall under one or other of the following:—

Variations due to Heredity.
     ,,   ,, Climate.

[1] Leighton, *British Serpents*, pp. 109, 110.

Variations due to Food.
,, ,, Locality.
,, ,, Age.
,, ,, Sex.
,, ,, Temperature.
,, ,, Moisture.
,, ,, Light.

It is quite obvious that in many of the instances of colour variation, two or more of the above factors will be exerting their influence concurrently. For example, the temperature and degree of moisture which form the environment of an animal depend upon its geographical distribution, *i.e.* the locality; while both these factors are part of all those which go to make up the climate. In like manner, what we term seasonal changes are associated with climate and locality. The old view that brilliancy of colour is dependent upon light and high temperature, is found to be unsatisfactory, since it does not follow that the animals of the hot and glaring desert present the brightest hues, and much of the deep-sea fauna is of very brilliant colouring, though living in comparative darkness.

But these considerations apply to the question of colour variation in its widest sense. When we come to consider the problem in a somewhat restricted area, many of the factors just mentioned are at once found to be inoperative to a great extent. In a country the size of Great Britain, it can hardly be supposed that climate can be responsible for any great extent of colour variation, since the variations in the climate in such a limited area are not sufficient. The same remark applies to some of the other factors, and, as a matter of fact, the list of those which are really responsible is found to be a comparatively short one. Fortunately, the problem has been very fully worked out in some countries which possess far more species of lizards than does Great Britain, and we may safely assume that the same factors produce colour variation in one family of lizards as in another. The colours themselves, of course, may be entirely different, and do not affect the question. We may therefore briefly note what has been observed in American lizards, where the number of species allows of more accurate conclusions being drawn than could be done from a restricted collection of our indigenous species.

The following examples of colour variation are quoted from Professor Cope's great work on *The Crocodiles, Lizards, and Snakes of North America*, a work which abounds in references to this question as affecting both snakes and lizards.

The genus *Sceloporus* consists of terrestrial, and therefore depressed Iguanidæ. Its especial habitat is Mexico and Central America, the south-western parts of the United States and California. The species are rather numerous, and in all the species the males are generally more brilliantly coloured and larger than the females; moreover, the males have a blue blotch on the under surface and on the sides of the belly. But while the species of *Sceloporus* possess brilliant colours, these are generally on the inferior surfaces and are therefore concealed. The throat and sides of the belly are usually of some shade of blue (sometimes purple), while the dorsal regions are, in the majority of species, different shades of brown. When the animal raises the head, as it habitually does, the brilliant colours of the throat are visible, but those of the sides are much less apparent. All these *colours are most conspicuous in the males*, and in many species they are absent from the females. They are to be regarded as secondary sexual characters. In the species *S. undulatus* the males are cross-barred, while the females are banded, the species being found all over the continent south of the Canadian district. In the species *S. dugesii*, the females resemble the males in the colour of the upper surface, but have the under parts yellow. In still another species of this genus (*S. pyrrhocephalus*) a marked distinction in colour is to be observed in the two sexes. The males are greenish brown with a broad black band extending from the shoulder to the groin, the sides being bluish. The females, on the other hand, have the head brown above, the lateral stripe is obsolete, and the blue marks on the sides are replaced by brown.

In several other species of the same genus we find a similar sex variation, the males exhibiting a blue colour on the chin and sides which is wanting in the females. In some other species the variations are still more striking, and Professor Cope thinks that *S. variabilis* was probably so named on account of the wide difference between the colouring of the males and the females.

Taking next another family of lizards, the Scincidæ, it is found that similar variations obtain in them. In some members the differences are so marked that they have been supposed to represent distinct species, but careful examination shows them to be attributable to age and sex. In these particular species (*Scincus erythrocephalus, quinquelineatus,* and *fasciatus*) Professor Cope says that it is probable, or even almost certain, that the females retain their stripes and other markings longer than the males, and have a much less tendency, if they exhibit it at all, to reddening and widening of the head. It is almost certain that females never entirely lose their stripes. All those of the largest size, with narrow head and distinct stripes, are females; all those of the same or even less size, with very broad red head and obscure markings, are males. Similar variations are found to characterise other species besides those named.

Examples such as those quoted might be multiplied almost indefinitely, but enough has been said to show that, from the point of view of *sex*, we have one powerful factor operating to produce colour variation.

The field naturalist will doubtless call to mind the fact that sexual colour variation is common in other

COLOUR VARIATION IN LIZARDS

animals than reptiles, notably in amphibians and birds. In the former we find amongst the newts some striking sexual colourings, while it is a matter of common knowledge that in the birds the sexes in very many cases are readily distinguished by the plumage.

Those who have studied this question in the reptiles will recollect that there is another factor which seems to exert considerable influence, and that is the factor of *age*. In the case of the adder it is found that the very old specimens are not so brilliantly coloured as are the young adults.[1] This applies to both sexes in those reptiles. The next point, therefore, is to inquire into the question of age in the case of the lizards.

Again, we may note some of the many observations on American species quoted in Professor Cope's book.

Referring again to the genus *Sceloporus*, the following instances of the effect of age strike the reader.

In the species *S. zosteromus* there is a dark, broad, lateral band connecting the groin with the arm in adults; in younger specimens the prebrachial spot often does not connect with the lateral abdominal band, the pigment in the intervening area apparently not having been yet developed. In *S. biseriatus*, the throat, middle of the belly, and lower side of the thigh may be black in old males, instead of the greyish or bluish colour of younger specimens.

[1] *British Serpents*, p. 120.

In the genus *Phrynosoma*, the so-called horned toads, a striking change of colour due to age is seen in the species *P. coronatum*. The young of both sexes have short tails. The colour above is brownish, yellowish, or greyish, darker laterally. There is a large brown patch on each side of the neck, and a series of three more or less distinct brown bars on each side of the back. These bars are light-bordered posteriorly. The tail is transversely banded with brown. The belly is often dotted or blotched with brown or black. *All these colour markings are more distinct in the young specimens than in old ones.* In very young individuals the scales on the top of the head are greyish or yellowish white, with a few minute brown or black spots. These spots, which are on the raised portions of the scales, become more numerous as the animals increase in size, *i.e.* in age, until the whole crown appears black or dark brown, crossed by irregular lines formed by the yellow posterior edges of the scales. So that in *P. coronatum* the colour of any particular specimen depends mainly upon the age. A closely related species exemplifies the disappearance of markings in old age, namely, *Anota platyrhina*. In this lizard the markings on the posterior part of the back are apt to become obsolete in old specimens. It frequently happens that the regular arrangement of the colour pattern is appreciable only in the young. An example of this is to be found in the Mexican *Heloderma suspectum*, a lizard of great interest, inasmuch as it has been by some supposed to be poisonous, whilst others have failed to detect any evidence of poison glands. If it be poisonous, it is the only genus that is so amongst lizards. The species noted is characterised by a series of rings on the limbs and on the tail. With increasing age these rings become broken up, and the pattern becomes an irregular coarse network of a blackish colour.

In the genus *Gerrhonotus*, the young individuals are much more brilliantly coloured than adults, and have a more distinct colour pattern of alternating light and dark cross-bars. On young individuals were proposed the species *G. cœruleus* and *G. webbii*. The colours fade out with increasing age and maturity in most species of this genus, becoming shades of olive or brown with lateral bars; or if the brilliant colours are retained as in two other species, *G. gramineus* and *G. auritus*, the cross-bars disappear.

Occasionally it is found that age is responsible for an apparently quite new arrangement of markings and colours, but, when this is the case, careful investigation shows that there are intermediate steps in the process as the age advances.

Thus, in the genus *Cnemidophorus*, a genus in which it is most difficult to discriminate the species, the colour markings differ in the same individual at different ages, and, what is still more interesting, the age at which the adult colouration is attained appears to vary in different localities. Some of the species, e.g. *C. sexlineatus*, never abandon the colouration of the young of other species and subspecies. When there is a distinct modification in colour marking due to age, the process is as follows:—The young are longitudinally striped from two to four stripes on each side of the middle line. With increasing age, light spots appear between the stripes, in the dark interspaces. At a later stage these spots increase in transverse diameter, breaking up the dark bands into spots. In some of the forms these dark spots extend themselves transversely and unite with each other, forming black cross stripes of greater or less length. Thus we have before us the process by which a longitudinally striped colouration is transformed into a transversely striped one, as age advances.

Another case in which the striped colouring of the young is replaced by spots in the adults and old specimens, is to be found in *C. tessalatus*, the process being similar to that just described.

We noted previously some sex variations in the Scincidæ. This family also exhibit striking variations due to age. Indeed, Professor Cope states that all the North American skinks lose their distinctive marks of colour with age. All are dark, nearly black, when young, varied with white lines or spots, which leave a trace of their presence when old. Three of the labials, the upper especially, are black with white centres. There is always retained a dusky border to the lateral edges. If the edge of the upper jaw be white, the

COLOUR VARIATION IN LIZARDS

character is never lost, the labials never having darker lateral borders. The light lines in increasing age generally remain for a time, and are bordered by blackish or dark brown, the interspaces generally becoming light olive. Even these, however, gradually disappear, and the scales generally are olivaceous above, with dusky borders, especially where originally dark coloured. The colour of the young in this genus is of great importance in classification.

In other skinks the light lateral lines of the young disappear entirely, and it is well known that the characteristic colour markings of the skinks are most appreciable in the young, the females retaining their markings longer than the males.

(References to other similar cases as those quoted are appended at the end of this chapter.)

If the reader will turn back to the chapters which described the colours of our indigenous lizards, he will see at once that the problem of colour variation in them is that of the whole group. The most striking differences are undoubtedly due to the two factors of age and sex. The very young specimens of *Lacerta vivipara*, the common lizard, are nearly black, while the adults are brown and spotted; the under parts red or orange in the males with black spots, while in the females these portions are yellowish. The young of the sand lizard, *L. agilis*, are greyish brown above with spots, whitish underneath; the adult male is typically green on the sides, the female more brown.

In *L. viridis*, the green lizard, the yellow lateral stripes which are found in the young persist in some of the old females, just as similar markings do in some of the skinks.

The general conclusion, therefore, is that colour variation in lizards is mainly to be accounted for by the influence of the two factors of age and sex. It must not be supposed, however, that these two factors are exclusively concerned in the matter, for many lizards exhibit variations which can only be explained by attributing them to individual peculiarities, whilst others, the sand lizard for example, have considerable *local* variations. The wall lizard, too, has a great number of colour varieties, some of which are undoubtedly local in origin, such as the variety on the Faraglione Rocks, near Capri, which is the colour of the rock on its upper parts, blue underneath. This is a matter of protective colouration, and it is in considering these varieties that the two questions of colour variation and protective colouration overlap. The object here, as we explained at the outset, has been to account for the variations found in a given species, irrespective of whether that species was protectively coloured or not. In either case, these variations are chiefly sexual or a matter of age, while some are due simply to individual peculiarities not affecting more than the particular specimen under observation.

For the benefit of those who would like to look more deeply into the matter, we append the following references to Professor Cope's work, from which this chapter is chiefly compiled.[1]

[1] *The Crocodiles, Lizards, and Snakes of North America*, by Edward Drinker Cope, Professor of Zoology, University of Pennsylvania. (Sex and colour, pp. 332-334, 336, 337, 342, 343, 400, 637. Age and colour, pp. 354, 357, 363, 382, 431, 445, 478, 508, 564, 569, 575-577, 627, 635, 636, 641, 642, 645.)

Other references :—

"Colour Variation in British Adders," *Proc. Roy. Phys. Soc.*, Edin., 1903. *British Serpents*, chapter ix. *Proceedings Dorset Nat. Hist. and Antiquarian Field Club*, vol. xxii. p. 43, 1901, Leighton. *Zoologist*, March 1892, Boulenger.

Since this chapter was written, Mr. Nelson Annandale has published his *Fasciculi Malayensis*. The report on the Batrachians and Reptiles collected by Mr. Annandale and Mr. Robinson has been furnished by G. A. Boulenger, and it is of great interest to find here also much evidence of the effect of *age* in the production of colour.

CHAPTER XIII

THE LIMBS OF LIZARDS

ORIGIN OF VARIATIONS—ORIGIN OF A LIMBLESS LIZARD.

THE widespread idea that the slow-worm is a snake and not a lizard is no doubt due to the fact that it possesses no visible signs of the presence of limbs. And as this absence of limbs is a characteristic feature of the serpents, the term "serpentiform" is used to describe those lizards which are likewise devoid of limbs, or partially so.

The oldest reptiles were possessed of the ordinary number of four limbs, constructed on the usual vertebrate pentadactyle type; it is only among recent forms that we meet with this singular departure from the vertebrate type of limbs, of which we have such a striking example in our indigenous slow-worm. In other words, limbless lizards have been evolved from lizards with four limbs, by a gradual process of reduction in size and number of limbs, and this reduction having been specially suited to some of the conditions in which reptiles are found, has become a fixed

THE LIMBS OF LIZARDS

character in certain families and species. The process is an excellent example of the origin of specific characters which the field naturalist may well be expected to be interested in, and we therefore propose to indicate very simply and briefly the views that are held on the subject, taking the slow-worm as an illustration.

The problem may be thus stated. Seeing that the earliest forms of reptiles were provided with limbs, and that at the present time a large number are limbless, what explanations does biology offer to account for this structural change occurring in the first instance, and becoming a fixed character afterwards in some species? Every field worker should be familiar with modern teaching on this question, and the group of lizards is a very convenient one in which to indicate the views held by various schools of thought.

For our purpose all that is necessary is to indicate the two main lines on which the explanations of such problems run, the older or Lamarckian view, and what we may describe as the modern or Darwinian view.

The underlying universal fact which has driven so many observers to give their attention to these matters is the great variation that is found everywhere in the animal world. The systematist gives expression to these variations by dividing animals into orders, families, genera, and species, according to their affinities and differences, thus emphasising the fact that some animals are closely related to others. But, further than that, it is a matter of common knowledge that no two animals are exactly alike, even the members of the same litter, except under very exceptional circumstances which we need not consider. Out of a litter of half a dozen puppies, some may resemble one parent, some another, some neither; while as they grow up to adult life entirely new characters may make their appearance in one of them. In other words, there is great variation even in closely related organisms. It is the question of what causes this variation in animals that gave rise to the two views above mentioned. How came the wonderful variety in shape, size, structure, and habits of all the species of animals? A paragraph in Mr. G. P. Mudge's *Text-book of Zoology* puts the matter as follows:—

"Biologists are divided into two great camps on the question of the 'Origin of Species.' There is the Lamarckian or older camp, and the Darwinian or newer one. The former asserts that organisms are profoundly modified by the necessities of their existence and the nature of their physical environment, and that these modifications are hereditarily transmitted, accumulated, and perfected with each generation. The Darwinian camp, on the other hand, asserts that variations are fortuitous, that they arise spontaneously from some inherent cause of which we know nothing, but that having arisen, they can be either advantageous or otherwise to the organism. If advantageous, then they confer a benefit and advantage upon the organism possessing them, which the others do not possess; and that therefore in the struggle for existence, the former will survive and procreate their species, and the latter will become exterminated. Thus Nature selects the fittest to survive, and rejects the unfit, and hence to the Darwinian theory has been given the name of Natural Selection. Thus may be explained why organisms are adapted to their environment; not because, as the Lamarckians assert, Nature has indiscriminately moulded them to it, but because those not so adapted have become exterminated."

It is no part of our purpose to even mention the various arguments for and against these opposing views, every field naturalist can and should become acquainted with them from zoological text-books. What we wish to do is simply to take the case of the slow-worm as an example of a species which has arisen as the result of variation, and apply the two views to it.

We may suppose that the ancient four-limbed lizard, according to the first of the views enunciated, found itself in the course of time, and in some circumstances of its distribution, under the necessity of taking to a burrowing life or living in loose sand, or in some other condition in which the limbs were not well adapted for locomotion. What the precise nature of the environment was does not matter. Whatever it was, "the organisms are profoundly modified by the necessities of their existence, and the nature of their physical environment." That is to say, that this lizard, *because of this environment*, became modified in structure, in the direction of the reduction in size of the limbs. These modifications "are hereditarily transmitted, accumulated, and perfected with each generation." The first lizards to have smaller limbs transmitted them to their offspring; the process continued; they in their turn were still further modified in the same direction, and transmitted their still smaller limbs to their offspring. The process is "perfected with each generation," until, finally, as the result of the effect of their environment, the lizard has no external limbs left at all. Thus a new species of lizard has arisen, without limbs, and at the same time some may be still in a transitional stage, with small limbs, or the hind pair only, showing the intermediate condition. We may represent the process diagrammatically thus:—

$$\left\{\begin{matrix}\text{Male (long limb)}\\ \text{have offspring}\\ \text{Female (long limb)}\end{matrix}\right\} \left\{\begin{matrix}\text{Male (short limb)}\\ \text{have offspring}\\ \text{Female (short limb)}\end{matrix}\right\} \left\{\begin{matrix}\text{Male (limbless)}\\ \\ \text{Female (limbless)}\end{matrix}\right.,$$

the structural change being due to—

(a) Action of the physical environment;

(b) Hereditary transmission of these acquired characters;

(c) Accumulation and perfection in succeeding generations.

It is to be particularly noted that according to this view the cause of the variation in the lizard is something extraneous to itself—its environment, in the first place, — and that the variation having once occurred, is transmitted by the influence of what is called heredity.

On the other hand, according to the Darwinian view, the initial factor in the variation of the four-limbed lizard is not to be sought for in extraneous circumstances such as environment, but in the inherent nature of animal life. All admit that the variations take place, but the newer theory is that these variations arise *spontaneously*. That does not mean that they arose in a haphazard way necessarily, but that they are the result of the operation of a law concerning which we know nothing. It means that it is the property of germ plasm to vary, whether the environment changes or not. The result of these variations may be useful to the creature or otherwise. In this case, if one of these spontaneous variations in the lizard took the shape of a reduction in the size of the limbs at a time when limbs were rather in the way than otherwise, then that variation would confer an advantage upon those individuals in which it occurred. If their life depended upon being able to burrow or otherwise protect themselves in some special way which limbs interfered with, it is obvious that the members of the race which had this new character would be the survivors in the struggle for life. If the circumstances which made this a useful variation continued in operation, those which had not thus varied would in time become exterminated. The offspring of the lizards with the reduced limbs would also have this character, some to a greater degree than others, and those in which it was most marked would in their turn survive. They would vary in their turn, and so the process would finally result again in a species of lizard without limbs. In this case the spontaneous variations have in some instances been adapted to the environment of the creature, and therefore have conferred upon it a commanding advantage, enabling it to survive where others have become exterminated. The environment has not caused the variation during the life of any given members of the species, but these members have given rise to offspring which have varied from their parents, simply because all offspring do vary more or less from their parents. They have thus become adapted to their environment, and given rise to a new species. According to this view, only a certain number of offspring possess the advantageous variation, and they are selected to survive. It only requires that a male and a female each possessed of the new character should pair, in order that it may be possible for the variation to become permanent and intensified. It thus appears that some very profound modifications may arise suddenly, as the result of this spontaneous variation, and in such a case the intermediate stages

THE LIMBS OF LIZARDS

may be non-existent. We may represent the origin of the limbless lizard on this view thus:—

{Male (long limbs), Female (long limbs)} offspring {Male (long limbs), Female (long limbs)} no variation; Female (short limbs), a spontaneous variation conferring an advantage.

If a similar variation arose in a male of the same or another litter, and the two spontaneous variations paired, the result would be—

Male (short limbs), Female (short limbs)} offspring a short-limbed family, a new species.

And similarly with other variations of kind or degree.

This brief outline of the two main biological views on this subject is merely intended to direct the attention of the field-naturalist reader to the explanations offered by science to account for the origin of such an anomalous reptile as the slow-worm is, as well as for the origin of species in general. It merely touches the fringe of the greatest of all biological subjects, and of necessity ignores all the numerous sidelights which may be thrown upon it; but it is hoped that it may be just sufficient to induce readers to examine the matter for themselves, and apply what they learn to the species of animals in their own country.

It remains to be noted what degrees of variation in the matter of limbs are to be found existing at the present day amongst lizards, which may be regarded as connecting links between the ordinary four-limbed type and the absolutely limbless species of which the slow-worm is an example.

It has been said that a burrowing habit, or a life amidst sand, might be regarded as conditions under which limbs would be not altogether an advantage, and, as a matter of fact, it will be found that it is precisely in those lizards which live under these conditions nowadays that this partial or complete absence of limbs is to be observed. It is, too, almost certain that the laws of the past in biology have been very similar in their methods of operation to those of the present.

Along with this reduction in the size of the limbs in lizards is found an elongated trunk or body, approaching the shape of that of a serpent. This is seen, for example, in the slow-worm. This long body may be associated with a shortened tail or not; in the slow-worm the tail is as long as the body. In many-limbed lizards the tail is, of course, considerably longer than the body, as in the viviparous lizard. Then we find that in the limbless lizards there are some vestiges of the limbs or limb girdles usually found under the skin. Those of the hind-limbs lie immediately in front of the anal aperture. A very interesting point is that the fore-limbs disappear before the hind-limbs, or are frequently smaller than the hind-limbs. Some species have hind-limbs only, while rarely the opposite condition occurs, *e.g.* in *Chirotes canaliculatus*, a species found in Mexico and

California, in which there are still fore-limbs with four clawed digits. This family (Amphisbænidæ) includes a number of species which are burrowing in habit and limbless; *Chirotes* being the only species with limbs. In most cases the pectoral and pelvic girdles are to be found in a vestigial condition; but in one family (Dibamidæ) not merely the limbs, but the limb girdles also are absent, though in the males there are flaps which seem to indicate limbs. The family to which the slow-worm belongs (Anguidæ) seems to be in a state of change, there being a general tendency to reduce and lose the limbs, which "may be more or less developed, or entirely absent externally, in which case, however, the rudiments of the pectoral and pelvic arches are always present" (*British Museum Catalogue*, G. A. Boulenger). Another member of the slow-worm family (*Ophisaurus apus*) possesses external rudiments of hind-limbs. This last species is of interest because the shape, arrangement, and number of the head shields are extremely similar to those of the slow-worm. It is known as the glass snake, and is found in South-Eastern Europe, South-Western Asia, and North Africa, growing to a length of 3 feet. Finally, in this connection may be mentioned the genus *Chamæsaura*, a South African genus, with three species which exhibit a curiously progressive diminution in the limbs which may be thus summarised:—

1. *C. ænea.*—Both pairs of limbs present, pentadactyle.

2. *C. anguina.*—Both pairs of limbs present, reduced to stumps (styliform and undivided).

3. *C. macrolepis.*— Fore-limbs absent; hind-limbs styliform, undivided.

A more gradual and complete reduction is seen if the whole of the genera in the slow-worm family be compared. Thus :—

SYNOPSIS OF THE GENERA IN THE ANGUIDÆ.

1. *Gerrhonotus.*—Limbs four, pentadactyle.
2. *Ophisaurus.*—Limbs absent, or hind pair rudimentary externally.
3. *Diploglossus.*—Limbs four, pentadactyle.
4. *Sauresia.*—Limbs four, tetradactyle.
5. *Panolopus.*— Limbs four, monodactyle or didactyle.
6. *Ophiodes.*—External rudiments of the hind-limbs only.
7. *Anguis.*—No trace of limbs externally.

Here we have in the one family a number of genera exhibiting a series of variations from the four-limbed five-fingered type to the highly specialised serpentiform creature without any external limbs at all, as in the slow-worm. It is the existence of so many intermediate conditions of organs that proves animals to be connected by almost every possible structural modification, and which makes it impossible to believe that species could have arisen except by a gradual transition of forms from the generalised type to the specialised, by means of natural selection acting upon ever-occurring morphological variations.

It naturally follows that locomotion in lizards will be of different kinds, according to the state of development or absence of limbs. The two extremes are, of course, the quick, running movements of the lizards with perfect fore and hind limbs, and the quiet, gliding motion of the entirely limbless forms, like the slow-worm. In intermediate forms the method of progression is likewise modified, sometimes exhibiting bipedal locomotion, the hind-limbs only being used. If the four limbs are very small in proportion to the body, the locomotion is correspondingly sluggish. Along with the variations in the limbs themselves there have occurred alterations in the muscular structures to enable the reptile to adopt the new mode of locomotion, and other organs have become similarly modified for their particular functions in the changed conditions of life.

It is only necessary to study the respective movements of different kinds of lizards to appreciate what a wonderful amount of specialisation has taken place in connection with this function alone, and the reader who would pursue this interesting topic is recommended to turn his attention to the geckos, skinks, and the slow-worm, to observe the immense variety of movements which have resulted from structural modifications. He will then naturally turn his attention to the question of the relationship of the lizards to the snakes, observing that in some families, that of the boa-constrictor for example, snakes have external indications of limbs in the shape of spurs, a subject which is beyond our province here.

The general conclusions to be drawn from an examination of all the lizards which exhibit some stage of degeneration in the limbs, are summed up by Professor Cope somewhat as follows. It is obvious that degeneracy of the scapular and pelvic arches to which the fore and hind limbs are attached when present, sooner or later follows partial or complete loss of the limbs themselves. In the Diploglossa (lizards with papillose tongues), the fore-limbs have disappeared more generally than the hind-limbs. In the skinks the limbs incline to degenerate more equally, the fore and hind limbs tending to be at the same stage. In one or two groups it seems that the fore-limbs have a tendency to persist longer than the hind-limbs. The scapular arch remains long after the degeneration and loss of the fore-limbs, before it degenerates itself, while the pelvic arch degenerates previously to the loss of the hind-limb.

The various parts of the scapular arch degenerate in the following order:—(1) limb; (2) interclavicle (generally); (3) costal attachment; (4) sternum.

The order of disappearance of the parts in the pelvis is:—(1) pubis and ischium together (generally); (2) limb; (3) ilium.

"The conclusion that the rudimental condition of

arches and limbs is due to degeneracy is supported by palæontologic evidence, which shows that the ancestral orders of the Reptilia (Cotylosauria and Theromora) had well-developed limbs. Similar evidence shows that the Sauria and Ophidia had a common ancestor."[1]

[1] Cope, *Crocodiles, Lizards, and Snakes*, p. 206.

PART II

BRITISH LIZARDS IN COUNTIES AND LOCALITIES

ARRANGED ACCORDING TO THE AREAS DEFINED IN THE

"COUNTY AND VICE-COUNTY DIVISIONS OF THE BRITISH ISLES"

(FOR BIOLOGICAL PURPOSES)

COUNTY AND VICE-COUNTY DIVISIONS OF THE BRITISH ISLES

(FOR BIOLOGICAL PURPOSES)

ENGLAND AND WALES.

C. CHANNEL ISLANDS.

I. PENINSULA PROVINCE.
1. West Cornwall with Scilly.
2. East Cornwall.
3. South Devon.
4. North Devon.
5. South Somerset.
6. North Somerset.

II. CHANNEL PROVINCE.
7. North Wilts.
8. South Wilts.
9. Dorset.
10. Isle of Wight.
11. South Hants.
12. North Hants.
13. West Sussex.
14. East Sussex.

III. THAMES PROVINCE.
15. East Kent.
16. West Kent.
17. Surrey.
18. South Essex.
19. North Essex.
20. Herts.
21. Middlesex.
22. Berks.
23. Oxford.
24. Bucks.

IV. OUSE PROVINCE.
25. East Suffolk.
26. West Suffolk.
27. East Norfolk.
28. West Norfolk.
29. Cambridge.
30. Bedford.
31. Hunts.
32. Northampton.

V. Severn Province.
33. East Gloucester.
34. West Gloucester.
35. Monmouth.
36. Hereford.
37. Worcester.
38. Warwick.
39. Stafford.
40. Shropshire.

VI. South Wales Province.
41. Glamorgan.
42. Brecon.
43. Radnor.
44. Carmarthen.
45. Pembroke.
46. Cardigan.

VII. North Wales Province.
47. Montgomery.
48. Merioneth.
49. Carnarvon.
50. Denbigh.
51. Flint.
52. Anglesey.

VIII. Trent Province.
53. South Lincoln.
54. North Lincoln.
55. Leicester with Rutland.
56. Nottingham.
57. Derby.

IX. Mersey Province.
58. Cheshire.
59. South Lancashire.
60. West (*i.e.* Mid) Lancashire.

X. Humber Province.
61. South-east York.
62. North-east York.
63. South-west York.
64. Mid-west York.
65. North-west York.

XI. Tyne Province.
66. Durham.
67. Northumberland, South.
68. Cheviotland, or Northumberland, North.

XII. Lakes Province.
69. Westmoreland with North Lancashire.
70. Cumberland.
71. Isle of Man.

SCOTLAND.

XIII. WEST LOWLANDS PROVINCE.
72. Dumfries.
73. Kirkcudbright.
74. Wigtown.
75. Ayr.
76. Renfrew.
77. Lanark.

XIV. EAST LOWLANDS PROVINCE.
78. Peebles.
79. Selkirk.
80. Roxburgh.
81. Berwick.
82. Haddington.
83. Edinburgh.
84. Linlithgow.

XV. EAST HIGHLANDS PROVINCE.
85. Fife with Kinross.
86. Stirling.
87. West Perth with Clackmannan.
88. Mid Perth.
89. East Perth.
90. Forfar.
91. Kincardine.
92. South Aberdeen.
93. North Aberdeen.
94. Banff.
95. Elgin or Moray.
96. Easterness (East Inverness with Nairn).

XVI. WEST HIGHLANDS PROVINCE.
97. Westerness (West Inverness).
98. (Main) Argyll.
99. Dumbarton.
100. Clyde Isles.
101. Cantyre.
102. South Ebudes (Islay, etc.).
103. Mid Ebudes (Mull, etc.).
104. North Ebudes (Skye, etc.).

XVII. NORTH HIGHLANDS PROVINCE.
105. West Ross.
106. East Ross.
107. East Sutherland.
108. West Sutherland.
109. Caithness.

XVIII. NORTH ISLES PROVINCE.
110. Outer Hebrides.
111. Orkneys.
112. Shetlands.

R. LLOYD PRAEGER'S FORTY DIVISIONS OF IRELAND (1896)

(See *Journal of Botany* and *Irish Naturalist* of February 1896)

IRELAND.

1. South Kerry.
2. North Kerry.
3. West Cork.
4. Mid Cork.
5. East Cork.
6. Waterford.
7. South Tipperary.
8. Limerick.
9. Clare with Aran Isles.
10. North Tipperary.
11. Kilkenny.
12. Wexford.
13. Carlow.
14. Queen's County.
15. South-east Galway.
16. West Galway.
17. North-east Galway.
18. King's County.
19. Kildare.
20. Wicklow.
21. Dublin.
22. Meath.
23. Westmeath.
24. Longford.
25. Roscommon.
26. East Mayo.
27. West Mayo.
28. Sligo.
29. Leitrim.
30. Cavan.
31. Louth.
32. Monaghan.
33. Fermanagh.
34. South Donegal.
35. North Donegal.
36. Tyrone.
37. Armagh.
38. Down.
39. Antrim.
40. Derry.

CHAPTER XIV

COUNTY AND LOCAL DISTRIBUTION

ARRANGED ACCORDING TO THE AREAS DEFINED IN THE COUNTY AND VICE-COUNTY DIVISIONS OF THE BRITISH ISLES (FOR BIOLOGICAL PURPOSES).

So far as I am aware no systematic effort has hitherto been made, or at any rate published, to show the relative frequency and distribution of the indigenous lizards of this country throughout all the counties. It therefore follows that the first attempt at such a description must be somewhat imperfect, and that there must be a good many blanks. It is quite impossible for one observer to work the problem out, and the method here adopted is similar to that in my previous work on the snakes. I have endeavoured to get information from most of the field clubs in the country on the point, and these reports have been condensed and tabulated according to the scheme before referred to. In addition to this, I have quoted the localities mentioned in the *British Museum Catalogue* as affording specimens, and some other records are obtained from other collections. In each case the name of the authority for the information is given opposite the record. The general results, as far as my present information goes, may be shortly summed up in a few paragraphs.

I. Peninsula Province.

Both the slow-worm and the common lizard occur frequently. The sand lizard is not found anywhere in this area, except, perhaps, on the Mendips.

II. Channel Province.

This is the best supplied of all the provinces in reptiles, snakes as well as lizards. The slow-worm is universally distributed throughout the province, including the Isle of Wight. The common lizard is likewise found everywhere in the province. In the New Forest it is called the Furze Evvet, in contradistinction to the newts, which are called Water Evvets.

The sand lizard, which is particularly characteristic of this province, along with its special enemy the smooth snake, is distributed locally on a few heaths. Bournemouth district, the New Forest heaths, and Wareham in Dorset, are the places most associated with this species.

III. Thames Province.

The slow-worm and the common lizard are found throughout the province, being perhaps more

COUNTY AND LOCAL DISTRIBUTION

numerous in Surrey and Kent than in the other counties.

The sand lizard is found in Surrey only, in the Farnham district, again associated with the smooth snake.

Years ago the smooth snake occurred in Berkshire in this province, and it is most interesting to note that it has recently (June 1903) been rediscovered near Wellington College, by one of the boys at the College. It is therefore quite possible that further careful search might reveal the presence of the sand lizard in Berkshire also.

IV. OUSE PROVINCE.

The slow-worm, though fairly common in places, is not so abundant as in the south and west of England. In some places it is quite unknown for miles. It is rare in the neighbourhood of Hickling. The author in 1901 took ten common lizards in this district in a few days, and only saw one slow-worm, which was brought to him from some distance. The common lizards are found on the sandhills on the coast particularly, where they are fairly numerous. The sand lizard does not occur.

V. SEVERN PROVINCE.

This province includes some localities which furnish abundance of slow-worms, especially in Gloucestershire, North Monmouthshire, parts of Herefordshire,

Worcestershire, and Shropshire. "The blind-worm is plentiful throughout Shropshire, in such situations as are suitable to its habits, and this too in spite of numbers killed every year by the misdirected zeal of ignorant persons" (*Fauna of Shropshire*, H. E. Forrest). The common lizard is not nearly so frequently seen as the slow-worm in most parts of the province, and in many parts there are areas of miles in extent in which it appears to be entirely absent. The author saw only one specimen in South Herefordshire and the Monnow Valley in seven years, whilst the slow-worm is very common in the same part. In other parts it occurs more plentifully.

In Shropshire, Mr. Forrest says of the common lizard that it is fairly common on heathy uplands. The provincial name is *Harriman*. Mr. J. Steele Elliot reports it as common in the Wyre Forest; and Mr. Martin Harding says he has seen it frequently along the old Potteries Railway line, near Shrewsbury (*Fauna of Shropshire*, H. E. Forrest, p. 189).

The sand lizard has been reported by several observers as occurring in Shropshire; but Mr. Forrest, who has carefully looked into the matter with Mr. G. A. Boulenger of the British Museum, has come to the conclusion that all these observers were mistaken, and that all the specimens supposed to be of the sand lizard species were in reality *Lacerta vivipara*. The great variation in colour has led to similar errors in other places.

VI. South Wales Province.

The slow-worm is common in this province, very numerous in some of the most southern localities. The common lizard is somewhat rare in Brecon and Radnor, and no information is available as to its occurrence elsewhere.

VII. North Wales Province.

The slow-worm is found throughout the province, as is the viviparous lizard. Our knowledge of the lizard distribution in this area is particularly complete owing to the researches of Mr. H. E. Forrest, who is preparing a work on the Fauna of North Wales. All the records quoted later for this province, though in the names of the individual observers, have been sent to me by Mr. Forrest for this work.

VIII. Trent Province.

In Leicestershire the slow-worm and the common lizard appear to be equally distributed in the large woods of the county, whilst in other parts of this area both species seem to be somewhat local in occurrence.

IX. Mersey Province.

The main interest in this area centres round the occurrence of the sand lizard in considerable numbers in the neighbourhood of Southport. In no district north of the Thames is this species so common as near

Southport. Its distribution is said to extend to the Cheshire coast also. The slow-worm and the common lizard both occur fairly numerously in restricted and specially suitable places.

X. Humber Province.

Here the slow-worm and common lizard are the only two species found, as in most of the northern provinces. Of these two, the information available points to the common lizard being the more common in the majority of places in the province. The slow-worm has suffered more than its more active relative at the hands of civilisation in these populous districts.

XI. Tyne Province.

On the whole the common lizard predominates over the slow-worm here also, though in some of the sheltered valleys the slow-worm is the more common. The latter species is, however, more local nowadays than the former.

XII. Lakes Province.

The author's experience of the Lake District has been that reptile life is conspicuous by its absence. No species can be said to be more than occasionally seen. The neighbourhood of Morecambe Bay is one of the localities where the slow-worm is fairly common. The common lizard occurs in the Isle of Man.

C. CHANNEL ISLANDS.

The only point that need be mentioned here is that the green lizard and the wall lizard occur in these islands as truly indigenous species. They should not be included in the fauna of any of the provinces of the mainland.

SCOTLAND.

The author has found both the slow-worm and the common lizard to be somewhat rare in the East Lowlands Province, certainly neither species is anywhere as common as in some of the English localities named. In the North Highlands Province he found the slow-worm rare, and the common lizard fairly common. Indeed, the latter may possibly be very common in the heather, since ten specimens were seen in as many days, and the colour protection of this species is so perfect that it may easily be much more common than is recognised.

There is no authentic record of the occurrence of the sand lizard in Scotland, though it has been reported. The specimen reported in *The Field* (July 11, 1903) as having been swallowed by an adder, was on more careful examination found to be the common lizard. (See *The Field*, July 18, 1903.)

IRELAND.

The statement that there are no reptiles in Ireland, though frequently made, is inaccurate, since the common lizard is found. The slow-worm is absent, else would the proverbial absence of snakes never have been recognised, as the popular fancy always is to regard the slow-worm as a snake. Some details of the distribution of Ireland's only reptile, the common lizard, are given later, and these have been furnished by Dr. Scharff.

COUNTY AND LOCAL DISTRIBUTION

REPORTS ON LOCAL DISTRIBUTION.

The following reports have been sent to the author from field naturalists in various parts of the country in reply to a circular asking for information on the local distribution of the lizards. The author takes this opportunity to express his thanks to all those who were good enough to supply this information or to obtain it from others. The reports are quoted *verbatim*, and the names and addresses of correspondents added for the sake of authority, and so that others interested may communicate with each other. The tables which follow are compiled from this list and from the specimens in various museums.

CHAPTER XV

I. PENINSULA PROVINCE. II. CHANNEL PROVINCE.

I. PENINSULA PROVINCE.

SOMERSET.

"THE slow-worm and the common lizard both abound. The sand lizard is found on the Mendips, where it has taken up its abode in the huge accumulation of fine sand, and the refuse of the lead workings, which have been carried on from very early times. I am not sure of its existence anywhere else in this neighbourhood."— HERBERT E. BALCH, Laura Place, Wells.

"The slow-worm is the most common in this district, the only other lizard I am acquainted with being the viviparous lizard, which I have seen in the neighbourhood of Glastonbury in the Mendip Hills, and at Clevedon. Slow-worms are common in all parts of the county as far as my observation goes."— ARTHUR BALLIED, Midsomer Norton.

"The slow-worm and the common lizard both occur in suitable localities in the district 15 miles round

Bristol (both Somerset and Gloucester), and are fairly common on Leigh Down and Brockley Common. The finest slow-worm I have ever seen was taken in Leigh Woods (Somerset) in May 1896, and measured 18 inches in length. Another, 16½ inches, was sprinkled with bright blue spots on the upper part of the neck and back of the body. These spots were irregular in shape and distribution, generally towards the outer edge of the scales. The effect was a beautiful colour variation."—H. J. CHARBONNIER, Kingsdown, Bristol.

[The blue-spotted colour is one which not uncommonly occurs in old specimens.—AUTHOR.]

DEVON.

"The slow-worm and viviparous lizard both occur, the latter being the most common. I have not found the sand lizard in Devonshire."—Rev. GREGORY C. BATEMAN, Lew Down.

"In South Devon the slow-worm is the most common, although the viviparous lizard is perhaps more often noticed, as the former frequents inaccessible places. The local names for these lizards vary in almost every parish."— E. A. S. ELLIOT, Kingsbridge, South Devon.

"In the Culm Valley the common viviparous lizard is the most numerous."—W. HORTON DATE, Culmstock.

II. CHANNEL PROVINCE.

HAMPSHIRE.

The following paragraphs relating to the lizards are from a paper on the "Reptiles of Hampshire and the Isle of Wight," by Rev. J. E. Kelsall (*Proc. Hamp. Field Club*, Part III. vol. iii. 1898):—

"The Slow-worm, or Blind-worm (*Anguis fragilis*).

"Universally distributed, including the island.

"This common reptile is well known to all country people. Though resembling a snake, it is really a lizard, with rudimentary limbs beneath its skin. It is quite harmless, and indeed useful, living chiefly on slugs. It brings forth living young.

"The Rev. H. M. Wilkinson, vicar of Milford, informs me that when living at Bisterne he once heard a disturbance amongst his poultry, and found that it was caused by a slow-worm, which had the tail of a young one hanging from its mouth. On killing it, he found several others in its stomach.

"The Common Lizard (*Lacerta vivipara*).

"Universally distributed, including the island.

"This is the common little brown scaly lizard, found upon all our dry banks and heaths. The forest people call it the Furze Evvet, to distinguish it from the Water Evvets or Newts. The natural history books call it the Scaly Lizard, or the Viviparous Lizard, because it does not lay eggs. When you try to catch it in the heather, it will sometimes run up the outside of your sleeve, and I have more than once carried one a long way clinging on to my coat or sitting on my shoulder.

"The Sand Lizard (*L. agilis*).

"Locally distributed; apparently confined to the Bournemouth and New Forest heaths.

"This is one of the rarer species referred to by Kingsley, who wrote of it as 'found on Bourne Heath, and, I suspect, in the South Hampshire moors also.' He probably counted Bourne Heath as belonging to Dorset. I have caught specimens at Bournemouth, but not yet in my own parish.

"The sand lizard is not always easily recognised; but if you see a *green* lizard, you may be sure it is this rarer kind. It is sometimes brown, but is larger than the common sort when full grown, and has three rows of spots down its back, each with a white centre. This lizard lays eggs, and is supposed to be the species referred to by Gilbert White as the 'beautiful green *Lacerti*' which he saw on the sunny sandbanks near Farnham."

"Both slow-worms and viviparous lizards are common in the New Forest." — MERVYN PALMER, Willmer Museum, West Norwood.

"In the Portsmouth and Gosport District Natural Science Society's area, the viviparous lizard and the slow-worm are common, the sand lizard being more local, but common where it is found. The two former species are more freely distributed. The district above referred to I have defined for cataloguing as starting from the mouth of the Tichfield river, through its course through Wickham, Droxford, to West Mean, turning east to Petersfield, and straight to the boundaries of the counties of Hants and Sussex, following this line to Emsworth, its termination. Thence through Chichester harbour, thence west through Spithead to Tichfield river. This embraces the watershed of the Tichfield river and Emsworth river, no river of any size being in this neighbourhood."—CHARLES FORAN, Normanton, Southsea.

HAMPSHIRE (HAYLING ISLAND).

"The slow-worm, the viviparous lizard, and the sand lizard are found in Hayling Island, the viviparous lizard being the most common."—A. MAY, Hayling Island, Hants.

SUSSEX.

"In my experience the slow-worm is the most common lizard; the viviparous lizard, though found, is not so common as formerly. I have never met with the sand lizard, though I believe it is found. The slow-worm is very abundant. The rustics look upon the common lizard as poisonous, and even educated people often regard the slow-worm as a venomous serpent."—B. LOMAX, 4 Cleveland Road, Brighton.

"The slow-worm is the most common, and usually looked upon as harmful. It is frequently met with in this locality. The common viviparous lizard is not so common here as on the Downs. Like the slow-worm and sand lizard, it does not hesitate to part with a portion of its tail, which by its wriggling about takes the attention of the pursuer off the escaping creature. The sand lizard is not uncommon here, although not so frequently seen."—JOSEPH ANDERSON, Alre Villa, Chichester.

"Both the slow-worm and the common lizard are very common in this district."—LESLIE LEWIS, near Arundel, Sussex.

DORSET.

"I have never seen any other lizard in the Weymouth neighbourhood but the slow-worm, which is very common. The viviparous lizard is very abundant near Parkstone."—NELSON M. RICHARDSON, Montevideo, near Weymouth.

"On April 28th, 1901, I captured a fine melanic variety of the viviparous lizard on Knowle Hill, near Corfe Castle."—E. R. BANKES (*Proc. Dorset Nat. Hist. Soc.*, 1902).

"The slow-worm, the sand lizard, and the viviparous lizard, are all found in Dorset; the viviparous lizard being perhaps the most common species."—H. J. MOULE, Dorchester.

The following extracts are from a paper on the "Reptiles of Dorset," by Rev. O. P. Cambridge, M.A.,

F.R.S., which was read before the Dorset Natural History and Antiquarian Field Club on March 15th, 1894. I am informed that it applies with equal truth to the present date.

"Sand Lizard (*Lacerta agilis*, Linn.).

"The length of this reptile often reaches 7 inches or slightly over. It is a beautiful species, and probably well known to most of our members who live in or near the heath districts. Its colour varies from bright green to dark rich brown, their hues being often intermingled in parts of the same individual, and always marked with numerous bright white or yellowish spots margined with black. In capturing this species care should be taken not to hold it by the tail, as it at once endeavours to get free by stiffening and snapping the tail off. A new tail will in time grow from the stump, but it is always of a more stumpy form than the original one, and its junction is plainly visible. I have frequently come across individuals with such stumpy tails, and have conjectured that they may have been lost in escaping from their enemy, the smooth snake (*Coronella lævis*), which appears to feed upon this lizard. (See *Proc. Dorset N. H. and A. F. Club*, vol. vii. p. 88.)

"This species may be kept alive in confinement. I have had them in a glass case, with heather and grass on its floor, for months together, feeding them with flies and other insects, and keeping a small saucer always full of water in the case, though I cannot say that I ever saw one drink. They are very pretty objects when basking in the sun, but with those kept in confinement I was not able to make any observations of much interest in respect to their ways and habits.

"The sand lizard is not a rare species in many parts of the Dorset heaths. As a rule, those examples found on the high and dry part of the heath are browner than those found in lower damp grassy parts; an evident adaptation to the surrounding colour, and no doubt protective.

"Viviparous Lizard (*L. vivipara*, Dum. et Bib.).

"The smaller size, more slender form, and duller colours of this lizard will easily prevent its being confounded with the preceding (*L. agilis*). As its name implies, it produces its young alive, not like the preceding, laying eggs which are afterwards hatched, but producing the young just after the shell (or rather membraneous envelope) bursts within the female. Its length is from 5 to 6 inches, and, although I have never found it in any abundance, it is not unfrequent in all the parts I have rambled over in Dorsetshire. It appears to be distributed generally through England, being also found both in Scotland and Ireland.

"Slow-worm (*Anguis fragilis*, Linn.).

"No description is needed of this common and (so

far as Europe is concerned) almost universally distributed reptile. Although destitute of limbs, it is in its essential characters nearer to the lizards than to the snakes. Though perfectly harmless, it is almost without exception disliked, and often superstitiously feared by English country folk. I have rarely come across a Dorset country person who would not, if it were possible, destroy a slow-worm. It varies considerably in size—from 10 to 14 inches—and, like the last species (*L. vivipara*), its young are produced alive." (End of extract.)

"All three species are found in the so-called Isle of Purbeck, which (in reality a peninsula) occupies the south-east corner of the county of Dorset. The most common is the viviparous lizard, found especially on the heaths and downs. The slow-worm is moderately common. The sand lizard has been very rarely found in the Isle of Purbeck, and then, of course, only on the heaths. I cannot remember having seen the viviparous lizard in those parts where the soil is stiff clay."—EUSTACE R. BANKES, Corfe Castle, Wareham.

"The most common species in my immediate neighbourhood is the green sand lizard. Among the snakes the smooth snake is not uncommon."—F. BECKFORD, Witley, Parkstone, Dorset.

WILTSHIRE.

"The slow-worm is quite common. I cannot say that I remember seeing either of the other lizards in the county of Wiltshire."—Rev. E. GODDARD, Clyffe Vicarage, Wooton Basset.

"The slow-worm and common lizard occur, the slow-worm most commonly. The common lizard is local, occurring, so far as I know, only in two or three places on warm banks."—E. MEYRICK, Elmswood, Marlborough.

ST. LEONARDS-ON-SEA.

"Each species occurs in the Hastings district, the slow-worm being the most commonly seen."—EDWARD CONNOLD, St. Leonards-on-Sea.

VARIOUS LOCALITIES.

"*The outskirts of Plymouth and Devonport.*

"*Anguis fragilis.*—Common.

"*Lacerta vivipara.*—Very common.

"*Pembroke Dock district.*

"*Anguis fragilis.*—Extremely common.

"*Lacerta vivipara.*—Also very abundant, particularly on a railway bank between Pembroke and Pembroke Dock. I have never seen these lizards so abundant anywhere else.

"*Portsmouth outskirts.*

"Have found the slow-worm only.

"*Falmouth.*

"I handled and released several slow-worms in May 1902.

"*Scilly Isles.*

"I saw two specimens of *Lacerta vivipara* in St. Mary's in August 1896.

"*Portishead, Somerset.*
"*Anguis fragilis.*—Fairly common.
"*Lacerta vivipara.*—Rather rare."—GEORGE BOYD, Stamford

CHAPTER XVI

III. THAMES PROVINCE. IV. OUSE PROVINCE.
V. SEVERN PROVINCE.

III. Thames Province.

OXFORDSHIRE.

"The slow-worm and the viviparous lizard both occur, and are equally common."—LILIAN VELEY, Hon. Sec., Ashmolean Nat. Hist. Soc., Oxford.

KENT.

"Both slow-worms and viviparous lizards are common here, the former especially. Both are giving way before the bricks and mortar; though both, I am glad to say, still occur on Bostall Heath. Two years ago (1901) I found eleven slow-worms on one Saturday afternoon ramble, on the edge of Plumstead Common. They were all under old tins, slates, etc."—ARTHUR S. POORE, Bostall Heath, Belvedere.

KENT AND SURREY.

"The slow-worm and common lizard both are found,

the latter most commonly. It is most abundant on heaths, as Hayes and Keston Commons, and in disused chalk quarries round Gravesend, where they sun themselves upon the pieces of chalk or stones. The viviparous lizard is easy to breed from the pregnant females. The slow-worm occurs occasionally in Lonesome Woods near Mitcham, also commonly under large stones on the South Kentish coast. In 1900 I took two, each 15 inches long, at Folkestone, one copper hued, the other steel grey."—MERVYN PALMER, Willmer Museum, West Norwood.

SURREY.

"All three species occur in Surrey. The slow-worm and the viviparous lizard most commonly. The sand lizard I find in a valley between the Devil's Jumps and Tilford; always fairly close to a delightful little brook that contains lamperns and crayfish. The sand lizard is very fond of grasshoppers as food."—OSWALD H. LATTER, Charterhouse, Godalming.

"The slow-worm is the most common. The sand lizard and the common lizard are found in about equal numbers upon the heath land of Fernsham and Hindhead."—BRYAN HOOK, Farnham, Surrey.

ESSEX.

"*Lacerta vivipara* and *Anguis fragilis* are both common in all parts of the county. They are our only local species."—HENRY LAVER, Colchester.

"The viviparous lizard is common at the sea-front at Southend."—MERVYN PALMER, Willmer Museum, West Norwood.

"The viviparous lizard is the most common, and the specimens found on the sand-dunes on the coast are very brilliantly coloured. It is possible that some of these brightly coloured specimens may be responsible for the records of the sand lizard which have appeared. On examination, all these have proved to be erroneous. It is a somewhat remarkable fact that the sand lizard should *not* occur."—WILLIAM COLE, Buckhurst Hill, Essex.

"I have records of the slow-worm from Ivor (Bucks), fairly plentiful at Hanwell (Middlesex), Chelmsford (Essex), Crockham Hill (Kent), and a number from Orlestone (Surrey). The viviparous lizard I know of from Burnham Beeches (Bucks), and Redhill (Surrey)."—W. M. WEBB, Odstock, Hanwell.

IV. OUSE PROVINCE.

NORFOLK.

"The viviparous lizard I have found fairly common on the edges of sand-dunes that extend from Yarmouth towards Cromer (Norfolk)." — OSWALD H. LATTER, Charterhouse, Godalming.

N.-E. NORFOLK.

"When reptile hunting in the neighbourhood of

Stalham I found the viviparous lizard common on the sand-dunes of the coast, but the slow-worm very rare. In fact, I saw only one specimen of the latter in a fortnight. Neither species seems common on the 'walls' round the broads."—AUTHOR.

V. SEVERN PROVINCE.

GLOUCESTER.

"The slow-worm and the viviparous lizard occur, the latter most commonly. A half-grown viper, caught in September, threw up the half-digested carcase of a common lizard shortly after being captured. I well remember noticing in 1884 that some viviparous lizards caught on the rubbly southern slope of Painswick Hill were of rather stronger build than those near Stroud, and had their scales seemingly more prominent, and certainly more polished."—CHAS. A. WITCHELL, Cheltenham.

"In the Cirencester district both the slow-worm and the common lizard are found, the former most often."—E. L. T. AUSTEN, Kingley, Alcester.

"The slow-worm and the common lizard both occur, but personally I have seen more specimens of the slow-worm than of the latter."—RICHARD P. LORD, Cirencester.

HEREFORD.

"In some parts of the county the slow-worm is very abundant, and attains a length of 16 to 17 inches. In the Monnow Valley the slow-worm is the only lizard I have ever seen, and the same remark applies to Garway Hill, Kentchurch, and Ewyas Harold. I am convinced from some years' observation that the viviparous lizard is very rare in South Herefordshire, while the slow-worm may be found in every old quarry."—AUTHOR.

STAFFORD.

"The viviparous lizard is the most common in this county. The slow-worm also occurs. The sand lizard has been once, but quite erroneously, recorded as being found in the county."—G. H. STORER, Burton-on-Trent.

SHROPSHIRE.

"The slow-worm is plentiful throughout Shropshire; while the common lizard, locally called Harriman, is fairly common on heathy uplands."—H. E. FORREST, Shrewsbury.

MONMOUTH.

"In North Monmouth the slow-worm is very abundant, especially in the valleys in the neighbourhood of the Graig Hill, and round Abergavenny. In these same localities the viviparous lizard is absent or at any rate extremely rare."—AUTHOR.

WORCESTER.

"The slow-worm seems generally distributed and moderately common throughout the county. The common lizard I have only seen in one Worcestershire locality, viz. Hartlebury Common near Stourport, a sandy common of considerable area covered with heather, gorse, etc. It probably occurs in other parts, but I have not personally observed it elsewhere, except in the Wyre Forest, where I remember seeing it some few years ago."—W. H. EDWARDS, Hastings Museum, Worcester.

The following extract is taken from the *Victorian History of Worcestershire* (vol. i. pp. 137, 138):—

"The sand lizard is met with in Worcestershire. Pennant gives Tenbury as a locality, and in parts of the Wyre Forest, and near Kidderminster, it is still to be found. The present writer received one, which was taken on the Worcestershire side of the park of Ragley, the seat of the Marquis of Hertford, which measured a little over 8 inches in length, and another of smaller size, which was captured when removing some rubbish at the entrance to the excavations for gypsum at Spurnal, near Alcester.

"Common or viviparous lizard.—Although so abundant in the southern counties of England, the present small species is rare in Worcestershire, or at any rate seldom observed, owing, no doubt, in some measure, to its unattractive appearance. There is, however, every reason to conclude that careful search would discover it in localities where it has not yet been noticed. On the Ridgeway, which divides the counties of Worcester and Warwick, this small lizard has been found, as well as on Hartlebury Common, and in Wyre Forest."

[I am not aware whether any of the specimens of sand lizards mentioned in the above paragraph are in existence, or whether they were authoritatively identified as such.—AUTHOR.]

CHAPTER XVII

VI. SOUTH WALES PROVINCE.
VII. NORTH WALES PROVINCE.
VIII. TRENT PROVINCE.
IX. MERSEY PROVINCE.
X. HUMBER PROVINCE.
XI. TYNE PROVINCE.
XII. LAKES PROVINCE.

VI. SOUTH WALES PROVINCE.

"I HAVE occasionally seen the common lizard, and it is probably more abundant than one would suppose, owing to the amount of 'cover' for it. The slow-worm is exceedingly plentiful. Both species are considered venomous by the country people in this district, an opinion which seems to be general in country places."—FRANK DAVIES, Newcastle-Emlyn.

BRECON.

"The slow-worm and the common lizard both occur, the former most commonly. The latter is rare, not nearly so often seen as in Sussex. The slow-worm is frequently seen."—Dr. W. BALDOCK FRY, Builth, Brecon.

CARDIGAN.

"The common lizard is abundant, and the slow-worm frequent, the former being most often seen. I have never identified the sand lizard here."—Prof. J. H. SALTER, University College, Aberystwith.

RADNOR, PEMBROKE, CARMARTHEN, CARDIGAN.

"The common lizard and the slow-worm are both found in the above counties, the slow-worm being the most common. Both may be seen in probably any locality in S. Wales. The slow-worm is commonly found resting under large slabs of stone, indeed I believe that if they can find such a place they will choose it in preference to any other. A favourite hunting-ground for boys used to be the churchyard, and underneath some fallen headstone three would often be found lying together."—J. HERBERT, Disserth Rectory, Llandrindod.

GLAMORGAN (EAST).

"The slow-worm, which is always called an adder here, is fairly common. Before the Government took possession there was a very handsome cream-coloured variety on the island of Steep Holm in the Bristol Channel, while on the Flat Holm there was only the ordinary coloured one."—Letter from the late JOHN STORRIE, A.L.S., to AUTHOR.

VII. NORTH WALES PROVINCE.

The distribution of the slow-worm and the common lizard in this area is given in great detail later, from the inquiries made by Mr. Forrest. Both species occur almost everywhere in greatly varying number and proportions.—AUTHOR.

VIII. TRENT PROVINCE.

LEICESTER.

"The slow-worm and the common lizard are perhaps equally common in the district of Charnwood Forest. I have not seen either of them elsewhere. The sand lizard is recorded for Charnwood Forest in 1843, by Mr. James Harley, a competent observer, but there is no later record. I have generally seen the slow-worms in the rocky parts of Charnwood, but others have been brought to me from Norfolk where there are no rocks."—F. T. MOTT, Birstal Hill House, near Leicester.

NOTTINGHAM.

"All the lizards are very uncommon in this county. I hear on reliable authority that the slow-worm is not uncommon about railway banks in the Worksop district. The viviparous lizard I have seen and taken on the Barrow Hills, Averton Parish, North Notts."—Rev. A. THORNLEY, F.L.S., South Leverton Vicarage.

UPPINGHAM DISTRICT.

"The viviparous lizard is rare, one specimen from Wakerley Woods. The slow-worm is not common near Uppingham, two seen at Wakerley." — C. R. Haines, Uppingham. (*Zool. Report* for 1901.)

LINCOLN.

"The most common is the viviparous lizard, which is plentiful within a mile from here, on a sandy bank on Langton Hills, near Horncastle. The slow-worm is fairly common, in damp meadows chiefly, near the Woodhall Moor, five miles distant." — J. Conway Dalter, Langton, Horncastle.

IX. Mersey Province.

"Report has it that the sand lizard was once common on Overton Hills, and I saw and took some there on Whit-Monday, 1903. It is common on the sandhills at Southport, and I have brought specimens from that locality. I have also a fine male and female sent to me from Soham. This lizard does not appear to care much for water, although, when I have sprinkled water on the growing grass in their cage, I have seen them repeatedly take off the globules, which suggests that in the wild state the dew is their natural beverage. They are seldom, if ever, found in damp situations, and mine avoided the water-basin kept in their cage.

"The viviparous lizard occurs locally in the neighbourhood of Birkenhead and Liverpool, also at Weston, where they are known as 'Swifts.' Unlike the sand lizard, I have repeatedly seen this lizard dip its tongue in water, and altogether it seems to have less antipathy to moisture than the preceding species.

"The slow-worm is common in the midland counties, and is reported to have been found locally in the Frodsham district. It is not uncommon in Mid-Cheshire, and is often found by the platelayers on the railway between Knutsford and Chester."— LINNÆUS GREENING, Warrington. (Extract from a paper read before the Warrington Field Club, 1885.)

[During the month of July 1903 I received six sand lizards and one viviparous lizard from the Southport sandhills, which were captured by Mr. W. R. W. Wakefield. This seems to point to the conclusion that the viviparous lizard is much rarer than the sand lizard in this district. The slow-worm is uncommon. —AUTHOR.]

CHESHIRE.

"I have seen a few examples of the slow-worm in Cheshire, but it is not common. It is, however, common at Colwyn Bay and the surrounding district. The common viviparous lizard I have frequently seen in the hilly and heather-covered parts of Cheshire, also near Mold, and on the coast of Anglesey. At one time I thought the sand lizard occurred with us, but I now find that I was mistaken."—R. NEWSTEAD, Grosvenor Museum, Chester.

LANCASHIRE, CHESHIRE, AND DERBYSHIRE.

"The slow-worm occurs in each county; the sand lizard in Lancashire and Cheshire, and the viviparous lizard also in Lancashire and Cheshire.

"*Slow-worm.*—In the cultivated districts this species is less common than formerly, owing to so many being cut to pieces by mowing machines; but in remoter places, *e.g.* the Derbyshire dales, it is still abundant. In Lathkill Dale we have seen a score in a day. Its local name in North Lancashire is 'Lang-worm' (*i.e.* Long-worm), which is also a local name for the grass snake.

"*Viviparous lizard.*—This species is becoming rarer on account of the breaking-up of the peat bogs, but may still be found wherever there is a stretch of bog or mossland. On Chat Moss, near Manchester, it is still quite numerous. The local names are 'Land Asker' or 'Ground Ask,' or more usually in this part of Lancashire 'Chucktail.'

"*Sand lizard.*—Occurs here and there along the Lancashire and Cheshire coasts amongst the sand-dunes. It is now most abundant in the neighbourhood of Birkdale. Neither of us has ever seen this species inland, but only along the coast-line. The local names for it are 'Sand Dragon,' 'Green Asker,' and 'Chucktail.'

"The word 'Ask' or 'Asker' is a universal name applied to all newts and lizards in the three counties by the country-folk, by whom all creatures of the kind are considered venomous."—R. STANDEN and J. R. HARDY, Zoological Dept., Manchester Museum, Owens College.

X. HUMBER PROVINCE.

YORKSHIRE.

"In the Scarborough district both the viviparous lizard and the slow-worm are found, the former being the more common. This species is generally distributed in all suitable localities, and in some, *e.g.* upon the Wykeham High Moor, is extremely abundant. Its local name is 'Ask.' The local name for the blind-worm is 'Slier-worm,' pronounced as spelt. Both are considered venomous by the country-folk; the latter species particularly is held in greater dread than the adder. The viviparous lizard, probably on account of its small size and active habit, is holding its own, but the slow-worm is becoming less abundant every year. In some districts, where fifteen years ago it was plentiful, it is now quite exterminated. I have seen a young slow-worm disgorge a lob-worm only one inch less in length than itself, an apparently quite impossible morsel."—W. J. CLARKE, Scarborough.

YORKS.

"The viviparous lizard is more common than the

slow-worm, though both occur."—OXLEY GRABHAM, M.A., Pickering, Yorks.

RIPON DISTRICT.

"The slow-worm and common lizard both occur."— C. CHAPMAN, The Museum, Ripon.

XI. TYNE PROVINCE.

DURHAM.

"The common or viviparous lizard is the most abundant, and is found in the quieter parts of the sea-coast, and also on the borders of the western moors. The slow-worm is frequent in damp woods and moist places, especially in the western portion of the county, being much rarer in the eastern districts."—J. W. FAWCETT, Satley, Darlington.

"In the Derwent Valley the slow-worm is the most common, and some good specimens have been found not more than a quarter of a mile from where I reside. One was taken on May 14, 1901, the size of which was 13 inches. I have not found the common lizard in the lower parts of the Derwent Valley, but have seen numbers of them in the higher reaches, where I have had some interesting experiences of this creature's ability to avoid capture.

"At a point about five miles south-west of Newcastle, many years ago, I frequently saw a species which I now feel certain was the sand lizard, but I mention it with all reserve."—W. Johnson, Byper Moor, Burnopfield.

DURHAM (AND PART OF YORKSHIRE).

"Both the slow-worm and the viviparous lizard are fairly well distributed in this district."—G. Best, Darlington.

NORTHUMBERLAND AND DURHAM.

"I see the slow-worm fairly often and the common lizard now and then, and as this is without keeping a special lookout for them I should suppose that both are moderately common."—E. Leonard Gill, Museum, Barras Bridge, Newcastle-on-Tyne.

XII. Lakes Province.

CUMBERLAND.

"The slow-worm and viviparous lizard both occur in Cumberland, both being fairly common, especially in the west district on the coast-line. The common lizard is most frequently met with on the moorlands round Seascale."—T. G. Mathews, M.D., Whitehaven.

NORTH OF ENGLAND.

"The common lizard is plentiful in suitable dry, warm localities. I have found it often in the neighbourhood of Morecambe Bay.

"The slow-worm is very local. It is rare in Westmoreland, fairly plentiful in the Appleby district, and used to be found not far from Carlisle in woods on the banks of the Eden."—G. W. MURDOCH, Bentham R.S.O.

LANCASHIRE (NORTH OF THE SANDS).

"The slow-worm is the most common, although it may be local, as the late H. A. Macpherson (*Fauna of Lakeland*, 1892) thought. In the neighbourhood of Ulverston I have seen only one specimen of the common viviparous lizard; but this proves nothing, as I can say the same of the grass snake, which other people have found locally abundant. On the limestones of West Lancashire I have seen no reptiles except a few vipers."—S. L. PETTY, Ulverston, Lancs.

CUMBERLAND, NORTH LANCASHIRE, AND WESTMORELAND.

"The most common is *L. vivipara*, which in many places is numerous. Dry sandbanks, hedgerows, and quiet roadsides are the special haunts. It may be seen sunning itself on the piles of old sleepers near quiet railway stations. *Anguis fragilis* is, I believe, in some parts of Furness more common than *L. vivipara*. I had no difficulty when living at Ulverston in finding small colonies of this species, often several individuals under one stone, about the edges of the high moorlands near there. In Cumberland and Westmoreland it is thinly scattered, nowhere in any great numbers."
—W. DUCKWORTH, Beaconside, Penrith.

CHAPTER XVIII

SCOTLAND

THROUGHOUT the whole of Scotland the slow-worm and the common lizard are both to be found, of course more plentifully in some districts than in others, but still the distribution of both species is almost universal. The author was much struck, during a recent reptile hunt in the Highlands of Ross-shire and Inverness-shire, with the comparative rarity of the slow-worm in the particular glens searched, whilst the common lizard was frequently seen scuttling away amongst the heather, and this experience seems to have been that of many other observers. On the whole, then, we may say that the common viviparous lizard is the most common in Scotland, and that the slow-worm is almost as widely—if less numerously—distributed.

SCOTLAND.

Mr. G. A. Boulenger, F.R.S., has been kind enough to send me the list of lizards and the localities from which they were taken, which are in the

British Museum at South Kensington. These are as follows:—

Anguis fragilis (slow-worm).
    Aberdeen.
    Loch Tay, Perthshire.
    Stornoway, Lewis Island.
Lacerta vivipara (viviparous lizard).
    West Ross-shire.

PERTH.

"The slow-worm and the viviparous lizard are found, the latter being the more common. It is widely distributed throughout the county, but nowhere, I think, very numerous, though one may sometimes see four or five in one day, while hunting the southern slopes of heather-covered hills during sunshine. I have only once taken the slow-worm, and but rarely have one sent to the Museum. I am not sure that they are so rare as might be supposed, their habit of moving about in thick herbage having much to do with their rare appearances."—ALEX. RODGER, Museum, Perth.

STIRLING.

"The common lizard is the more numerous. The slow-worm is also common, though not so often found. I have not seen any slow-worms on this estate, but I have in Torwood and west of Stirling, and once on Kippen Moss. I think they are to be found on

Dunmore and on Airth Sounds close to the Firth of Forth.

"As regards Scotland in general, I should describe the distribution of both species as almost universal, and the excepted of more interest than the occupied localities. I can scarcely name a county in Scotland which I have visited in which they are not to be met with, and they are common even on the isolated rock of Ailsa Craig. In Harris and Lewis they swarm. I have seen them all over Sutherland. I have not seen them in Orkney nor Shetland. The colouring of the slow-worm which I saw on Ailsa Craig was brown-steel colour; such as I have seen in Sutherland are blue-steel colour."—J. A. HARVIE-BROWN, Dunipace, Larbert.

"The common lizard or 'Ask' is generally distributed throughout the west of Scotland in dry heathy places, stone heaps, walls, and ruined buildings.

"The slow-worm is very common amongst dead wood and decayed leaves, quarry refuse, and stone heaps, preferring dry situations.

"The obscure and retiring habits of these creatures induce people to believe that they are individually scarce. This is far from being the case, as they may still be found fairly numerously in spite of the relentless persecution to which they are subjected."—MSS. of the late Mr. ALFRED LUSS, Dumbarton.

"The slow-worm and the viviparous lizard may be called frequent in all the following counties:—Lanark, Renfrew, Ayr, Stirling, Argyll, Dumbarton, and Bute.

In most, the viviparous lizard is the more common. In Ailsa Craig, however, the slow-worm *was* very common, and attained a large size. I have frequently found them 18 inches long. Since the introduction of the rat, they are far less common, and likely soon to be scarce from the depredations of that rodent. Their favourite food seems to be snails, and the ease with which they can swallow the larger black slugs so common on the Craig is marvellous. The slow-worm is common all over Arran, where it is called in many places the 'Silver Adder,' and ruthlessly destroyed by the people as venomous. Their favourite spot is under flattish stones where there is a cavity underneath, and in moderately dry or porous soil.

"In a field, formerly a marsh, at Dunoon, now being converted into a public park, the viviparous lizard was very common among the furze bushes, among the roots of which, in sunny spots, the gravid female would often be seen basking in the sun. I have also seen this species close to the summit of Ailsa Craig, where, however, it is less common than the slow-worm. Being more active and shy than the latter, it is less likely to be observed unless one is on the lookout for them."—J. MACKNAUGHT CAMPBELL, Kelvingrove Museum, Glasgow.

Mr. W. Eagle Clarke, F.R.S.E. (Science and Art Museum, Edinburgh), has sent me the following extracts from his records of specimens which have come under his notice at the Museum.

"*Lacerta vivipara.*—A specimen examined from Morven, Sound of Mull, Argyll, June 1893. A young specimen brought alive which had been captured in Arran, September 3, 1888. Two specimens from the Island of Rum, Hebrides, captured by Mr. Symington Grieve and brought for identification, July 1884.

"*Anguis fragilis.*—A specimen sent by Charles Campbell from Morven, Sound of Mull, June 6, 1893. Another from same place, July 19, 1893, measured 300 mm. One captured in June 1897, in East Princes Street Gardens, brought alive. I have also had it alive from Arthur's Seat. Several correspondents in the *Evening Dispatch,* May 1896, speak of the slow-worm as not uncommon on Blackford Hill.

"*L. agilis.*—On October 8, 1895, I examined the specimen of the sand lizard belonging to the Elgin Museum. It was from Culbin Sands, and proved to be only a medium-sized example of the common lizard (*L. vivipara*). This is the specimen upon which the species has been included in the fauna of Scotland."

Mr. Wm. Evans, F.R.S.E., Edinburgh, has been good enough to send me the following note and extracts from his observations in various Scottish districts.

"In my experience the common viviparous lizard is the commoner and more generally distributed in Scotland. The following notes are additional to my paper published by the Royal Physical Society in 1894 (vol. xii.):—

"Slow-worm, *A. fragilis.*—In 1897 a slow-worm was captured in East Princes Street Gardens, Edinburgh, and is recorded in the *Annual Report of the Museum of Science and Art* for that year.

"On April 11, 1901, my son, Mr. W. Edgar Evans, saw a party of youths kill one on the south side of Blackford Hill, Edinburgh.

"On August 20, 1894, I received a male from Doune, S.W. Perthshire.

"In April 1896, I found the slow-worm to be fairly common around Aberfoyle, on the confines of the counties of Perth and Stirling. On April 19, one was observed basking in the sun along with three adders on a bank near Loch Ard, Aberfoyle. So closely were they all huddled together and mixed up before being disturbed by me, that little more than the head of the slow-worm could be made out. I secured one of the adders, and then tried to capture the slow-worm, but it escaped minus its tail.

"In May 1897, I again met with a few slow-worms about Aberfoyle.

"On September 11, 1897, one was captured at Denny, Stirlingshire, and taken to Mr. Harvie-Brown.

"In May 1893, I came upon one at Loch Vaa, near Aviemore, Inverness-shire.

"In July 1901, two adult slow-worms, a male and a female—the latter 15 inches long—were brought to me from Loch Awe, Argyllshire. They were put into a fern case, and on July 29 two young ones were discovered beside them. The female seemed still as bulky as before, but next day she was much thinner, and my son then took from among the moss in the case no less than twelve young ones. The length of these was about 3 inches, colour pale yellowish, grey on upper surface and sides, under surface black, and a black spot on forepart of head, and another larger one on occiput, with a line running backwards from it.

"Common lizard, *L. vivipara.*—Two from Bavelaw Moss, near Balerno, Midlothian, April 1898. Another, a young very dark specimen in same locality, August 22, 1901.

"In June 1895, I received a female from Craigburn Quarry, Peeblesshire; and on April 7, 1896, another from Eddleston in the same county.

"In April and May 1896, I found this species commonly about Aberfoyle, S.W. Perthshire.

"In September 1891, I observed several at Cromdale, Strathspey, Elginshire, and, in May 1893, two or three near Aviemore, Inverness.

"In April 1894, I found it locally common in the vicinity of Oban, Argyllshire.

"In September 1900, I saw several at Elvanfoot, Lanarkshire. One of these I captured alive, but not before it had parted with its tail, which wriggled about on the ground for a considerable time. The stump bled a little, but not much. After photographing the animal it was set at liberty."—WM. EVANS, Morningside, Edinburgh.

CHAPTER XIX

IRELAND

MR. G. A. BOULENGER informs me that the Irish specimens in the British Museum are as follows:—
Lacerta vivipara (viviparous lizard).
    County Meath.
    Graigue, Kilkenny.

Dr. R. Scharff, Science and Art Museum, Dublin, has sent me the following paragraph:—

"The viviparous lizard (*L. vivipara*), though widely spread in Ireland, is decidedly rare and almost unknown to the general public. We possess specimens in this Museum from the following localities:—

Kenmare, Co. Kerry.	Bellmullet, Co. Mayo.
Killarney, Co. Kerry.	Moville, Co. Donegal.
Castletown-Berehaven, Co. Kerry.	Piperstown, Co. Louth.
	Feltrim Hill, Co. Dublin.
Roundstone, Co. Galway.	Glen of the Downs, Co. Wicklow.
Cappagh, Co. Waterford.	

"I have no doubt at all that this species occurs in every county in Ireland. Thompson (cf. *Natural History of Ireland*) records it from Co. Down, Antrim, and Cork. Most of the specimens in this Museum I collected myself when looking for mollusca under stones or in hedges."

We may therefore state that the viviparous lizard is generally distributed throughout Ireland, although not abundantly as regards the numbers in a particular locality.

CHAPTER XX

SUMMARY OF COUNTY AND DISTRICT DISTRIBUTION

THE following records have been obtained for the provinces:—

I. PENINSULA PROVINCE.

1. West Cornwall with Scilly.
2. East Cornwall.
3. South Devon.
4. North Devon.
5. South Somerset.
6. North Somerset.

Slow-worm, *Anguis fragilis.*

LOCALITY.	FREQUENCY.	OBSERVER.
Somerset	Abundant	H. E. Balch.
Midsomer Norton	Common	A. Ballied.
Devon	Not uncommon	Rev. G. C. Bateman.
South Devon	Common	E. A. Elliot.
Bristol (district)	Fairly common	H. Charbonnier.

Common Lizard, *Lacerta vivipara.*

Devon	Plentiful	H. P. Hearder.
Falmouth (Cornwall)	...	Spec. Brit. Mus.
Fowey (Cornwall)	...	,, ,,
Devon	Common	Rev. G. C. Bateman.
Bristol (district)	Fairly common	H. Charbonnier.

Sand Lizard, *Lacerta agilis*.

LOCALITY.	FREQUENCY.	OBSERVER.
Mendip Hills	Occurs	H. Balch.

II. CHANNEL PROVINCE.

7. North Wilts.
8. South Wilts.
9. Dorset.
10. Isle of Wight.
11. South Hants.
12. North Hants.
13. West Sussex.
14. East Sussex.

Slow-worm, *Anguis fragilis*.

LOCALITY.	FREQUENCY.	OBSERVER.
Central Dorset	Common	Dr. Leighton.
Isle of Wight	,,	Rev. J. E. Kelsall.
Hampshire	Universal	,, ,,
Dorset	Common	Rev. O. P. Cambridge.
Central Dorset	,,	Rev. F. W. Brandreth.
Ringwood	...	Spec. Brit. Mus.
Crowborough (Sussex)	...	,, ,,
Sussex	Abundant	B. Lomax.
New Forest	Common	M. Palmer.
Weymouth	Very common	N. Richardson.
Wiltshire	Common	Rev. E. Goddard.

Common Lizard, *Lacerta vivipara*.

Central Dorset	Fairly common	Dr. Leighton.
Dorset	Not uncommon	Rev. O. P. Cambridge.
Hampshire	Universal	Rev. J. E. Kelsall.
Isle of Wight	,,	,, ,,
Eastbourne	...	Spec. Brit. Mus.
Ringwood	...	,, ,,
Bournemouth	...	,, ,,
Poole Heath	...	,, ,,
Petersfield (Hants)	...	,, ,,

Sand Lizard, *Lacerta agilis*.

LOCALITY.	FREQUENCY.	OBSERVER.
Dorset heaths	Not rare	Rev. O. P. Cambridge.
Bournemouth	Local	Rev. J. E. Kelsall.
New Forest	,,	,, ,,
Poole Heath	...	Spec. Brit. Mus.
Bournemouth	...	,, ,,
Ringwood	...	,, ,,
Stutland Heath (near Swanage)	...	,, ,,

III. THAMES PROVINCE.

15. East Kent.
16. West Kent.
17. Surrey.
18. South Essex.
19. North Essex.
20. Herts.
21. Middlesex.
22. Berks.
23. Oxford.
24. Bucks.

Slow-worm, *Anguis fragilis*.

LOCALITY.	FREQUENCY.	OBSERVER.
Knockholt (Kent)	...	Spec. Brit. Mus.
Oxted (Surrey)	...	,, ,,
Mitcham (near)	Occasional	M. Palmer.
South Kent	Common	,,
Bostall Heath (Kent)	Occurs	A. Poore.
Plumstead Common (Kent)	Common	,,
Essex	,,	H. Laver.
Iver (Bucks)	Occurs	W. Webb.
Hanwell (Middlesex)	Fairly plentiful	,,
Chelmsford (Essex)	,, ,,	,,
Crockham Hill (Kent)	,, ,,	,,
Orlestone (Surrey)	,, ,,	,,

Common Lizard, *Lacerta vivipara*.

Limpsfield (Surrey)	...	Spec. Brit. Mus.
Sheire Common (Surrey)	...	,, ,,

Locality.	Frequency.	Observer.
Hayes Common	Abundant	M. Palmer.
Keston Common	,,	,,
Gravesend (near)	,,	,,
Bostall Heath (Kent)	Occurs	A. Poore.
Essex	Common	H. Laver.
Southend	,,	M. Palmer.

Sand Lizard, *Lacerta agilis*.

Farnham Common (Surrey)	...	Spec. Brit. Mus.
Tilford (near), Surrey	Occurs	Oswald Latter.

IV. OUSE PROVINCE.

25. East Suffolk. 29. Cambridge.
26. West Suffolk. 30. Bedford.
27. East Norfolk. 31. Hunts.
28. West Norfolk. 32. Northampton.

Slow-worm, *Anguis fragilis*.

Locality.	Frequency.	Observer.
N.E. Norfolk	Rare	Dr. Leighton.

Common Lizard, *Lacerta vivipara*.

N.E. Norfolk	Common	Dr. Leighton.
Norfolk	...	Spec. Brit. Mus.
Cromer (near)	Fairly common	O. Latter.

V. SEVERN PROVINCE.

33. East Gloucester. 37. Worcester.
34. West Gloucester. 38. Warwick.
35. Monmouth. 39. Stafford.
36. Hereford. 40. Shropshire.

Slow-worm, *Anguis fragilis.*

LOCALITY.	FREQUENCY.	OBSERVER.
N. Monmouth	Common	Dr. Leighton.
Monnow Valley	,,	,,
South Hereford	Very common	,,
Welsh Newton	Fairly common	,,
Wye Valley	Common	,,
Forest of Dean	,,	,,
South Shropshire	Plentiful	H. E. Forrest.
North Shropshire	Fairly common	,,
Gloucester	Common	C. Witchell.
Stafford	Occurs	G. H. Storer.
Cirencester	Common	E. Austen.

Common Lizard, *Lacerta vivipara.*

N. Monmouth	Rare	Dr. Leighton.
S. Hereford	,,	,,
Monnow Valley	Very rare	,,
Shropshire heaths	Fairly common	H. E. Forrest.
Wyre Forest	Common	J. Steele Elliot.
Shrewsbury (near)	Frequent	Martin J. Harding.
Church-Stretton district	Common	H. E. Forrest.
Gloucester	,,	C. Witchell.
Stafford	,,	G. H. Storer.
Cirencester	Occurs	E. Austen.
Hartlebury (Worcester)	Common Seen	W. Edwards.

VI. SOUTH WALES PROVINCE.

41. Glamorgan. 44. Carmarthen.
42. Brecon.   45. Pembroke.
43. Radnor.   46. Cardigan.

Slow-worm, *Anguis fragilis.*

LOCALITY.	FREQUENCY.	OBSERVER.
Cardigan	Common	Prof. J. H. Salter.
Newcastle-Emlyn	Abundant	F. Davies.
Brecon	Frequent	Dr. Fry.

Common Lizard, *Lacerta vivipara*.

LOCALITY.	FREQUENCY.	OBSERVER.
Aberystwith	Abundant	Prof. J. H. Salter.
Cardigan	,,	,, ,,
Brecon	Occurs	Dr. Fry.
Newcastle-Emlyn	,,	F. Davies.

VII. NORTH WALES PROVINCE.

47. Montgomery.   50. Denbigh.
48. Merioneth.   51. Flint.
49. Carnarvon.   52. Anglesey.

Slow-worm, *Anguis fragilis*.

	LOCALITY.	FREQUENCY.	OBSERVER.
47.	Welshpool	Common	Miss Mytton.
	Leighton	,,	Miss Naylor.
	Montgomery	Scarce	Rev. E. W. Brown.
	Forden	Occurs	Rev. J. E. Vize.
	Newtown	Plentiful	E. J. Williams.
	Llanerfyl	,,	Rev. C. Harington.
	Carno	,,	Mrs. Andrew Davies.
48.	Bala	Common	T. Ruddy.
	Corris	Seen	F. H. Birley.
	Aberdovey	Common	W. E. E. Kershaw.
	Towyn	,,	E. W. Kirkby.
	Barmouth	,,	F. C. Rawlings.
	Llanbedr	Clusters found when digging in spring of 1902	A. Moore.
	Penrhyn Deudraeth	Common	A. B. Priestley.
49.	Bangor	,,	Dr. P. J. White.
	Conway	,,	A. Moore.
	Deganwy	,,	G. A. Hutchinson.
	Llanberis	,,	W. H. Brinckman.
	Nanhoron (near Aberdaron)	Very numerous	C. Lloyd Edwards.

COUNTY AND DISTRICT DISTRIBUTION 201

LOCALITY.	FREQUENCY.	OBSERVER.
49. Menai Straits	Plentiful	E. G. Humphreys.
50. } Mold 51. }	,,	Col. Davies Cooke.
Colwyn Bay	Fairly common	R. Newstead.
Llanrwst	Plentiful	W. B. Halhed.
Llangollen	,,	J. Pownall.
Llansilin	Scarce	G. Dumville Lees.
Wrexham	Common but diminishing	R. H. Venables Kyrke.
52. Menai Bridge	Common	Dr. P. J. White.
Llandegfan	,,	J. Rowland.
Pentraeth	Observed 1902	C. Oldham.
Aberffraw	Few seen	E. Gosling.
Holyhead	Rather scarce	R. J. Edwards.

Common Lizard, *Lacerta vivipara*.

47. Welshpool	Plentiful	P. A. Beck.
Leighton	,,	F. Williams.
Montgomery	Scarce	Rev. E. W. Brown.
Forden	Occurs	Rev. J. E. Vize.
Newtown	Plentiful	E. J. Williams.
Llanerfyl	,,	Rev. C. Harington.
Carno	,,	Mrs. Andrew Davies.
48. Bala	Common	T. Ruddy.
Aberdovey	,,	W. E. E. Kershaw.
Towyn	,,	E. W. Kirkby.
Llanbedr	,,	A. Moore.
Penrhyn Deudraeth	,,	A. B. Priestley.
49. Bangor	,,	E. G. Humphreys.
Conway	,,	A. Moore.
Deganwy	In stone walls	T. H. Hague.
Llanberis	Common	W. H. Brinckman.
Nanhoron	,,	C. Lloyd Edwards.
Ffestiniog	,,	H. E. Forrest.
50. } Mold 51. }	{ Common on limestone rocks }	Col. Davies Cooke.
Colwyn Bay	Fairly common	Dr. W. B. Russell.
Llanrwst	Plentiful	W. B. Halhed.
St. Asaph	Common	W. A. Rogers.
Wrexham	,, on moors	R. H. Venables Kyrke.

LOCALITY.	FREQUENCY.	OBSERVER.
52. Menai Straits	Common	E. G. Humphreys.
Llandegfan	,,	J. Rowland.
Rhosneigr	,,	Col. T. Long.
Holyhead	,,	R. J. Edwards.

VIII. TRENT PROVINCE.

53. South Lincoln.   56. Nottingham.
54. North Lincoln.   57. Derby.
55. Leicester with Rutland.

Slow-worm, *Anguis fragilis*.

LOCALITY.	FREQUENCY.	OBSERVER.
Woodhall Moor (Lincoln)	Occurs	J. Conway Dalter.
Uppingham	Not common	R. Haines.
Leicester (Charnwood)	Common	F. T. Mott.
Derbyshire dales	Abundant	R. Standen.

Common Lizard, *Lacerta vivipara*.

Langton Hills (Lincoln)	Plentiful	J. Conway Dalter.
Uppingham	Rare	R. Haines.
Charnwood Forest (Leicester)	Common	F. T. Mott.

IX. MERSEY PROVINCE.

58. Cheshire.   59. South Lancashire.
60. West (*i.e.* Mid) Lancashire.

Slow-worm, *Anguis fragilis*.

LOCALITY.	FREQUENCY.	OBSERVER.
Newby Bridge (Lancs.)	...	Spec. Brit. Mus.
Mid-Cheshire	Not uncommon	Lin. Greening.
Knutsford	,,	,,
Chester	,,	,,

Common Lizard, *Lacerta vivipara*.

LOCALITY.	FREQUENCY.	OBSERVER.
Birkenhead } district Liverpool	Occurs	Lin. Greening.
Chat Moss (near Manchester)	Numerous	R. Standen.

Sand Lizard, *Lacerta agilis*.

Southport	Fairly common	Dr. Leighton.
Southport	...	Spec. Brit. Mus.
Overton Hill	Occurs	Lin. Greening.

X. HUMBER PROVINCE.

61. South-east York.   63. South-west York.
62. North-east York.   64. Mid-west York.
65. North-west York.

Slow-worm, *Anguis fragilis*.

LOCALITY.	FREQUENCY.	OBSERVER.
Scarborough (district)	Occurs	W. J. Clarke.
Ripon (district)	,,	C. Chapman.

Common Lizard, *Lacerta vivipara*.

Yorkshire	Fairly common	Oxley Grabham.
Scarborough (district)	,, ,,	W. J. Clarke.
Wykeham High Moor	Abundant	,,
Ripon (district)	Occurs	C. Chapman.

XI. TYNE PROVINCE.

66. Durham.   67. Northumberland, South.
68. Cheviotland, or Northumberland, North.

Slow-worm, *Anguis fragilis.*

LOCALITY.	FREQUENCY.	OBSERVER.
Durham	Fairly common	G. Best.

Common Lizard, *Lacerta vivipara.*

Durham	Fairly common	G. Best.

XII. LAKES PROVINCE.

69. Westmoreland with North Lancashire.
70. Cumberland.   71. Isle of Man.

Slow-worm, *Anguis fragilis.*

LOCALITY.	FREQUENCY.	OBSERVER.
West Durham	Frequent	J. Fawcett.
East Durham	Rarer	,,
Cumberland	Fairly common	T. G. Mathews.

Common Lizard, *Lacerta vivipara.*

West Durham	Frequent	J. Fawcett.
Cumberland	Fairly common	T. G. Mathews.
Isle of Man	Occurs	Dr. Leighton.

APPENDIX

THE following blank pages are intended to be filled up by the field naturalist as specimens come under observation, thus providing a permanent record of the distribution of our indigenous lizards additional to that recorded in the text, and a means of comparison with the observations of others.

[The author would be glad if field naturalists would from time to time communicate the results thus obtained to him.]

APPENDIX

ANGUIS FRAGILIS, or SLOW-WORM.

LOCALITY.	DATE.	OBSERVER.

LACERTA VIVIPARA, or COMMON LIZARD.

LOCALITY.	DATE.	OBSERVER.

APPENDIX

LACERTA AGILIS, or SAND LIZARD.

Locality.	Date.	Observer.

INDEX

The names of Counties, Districts, and Localities will be found under the heading "County Distribution."

The detailed references to the various species will be found under the respective headings "Slow-worm," "Common Lizard," "Sand Lizard," "Green Lizard," and "Wall Lizard."

ADDER, 41.
Anal scales, 15.
Anatomy of lizards, 14-23.
Anguis fragilis, 28-44.
Appendix, 205-208.
Asker, 181, 182.

BIOLOGICAL sheet, 145.
Bladder, 18.
Blind-worm, 24-44.
Blunt tail, 33.

CHUCKTAIL, 181.
Class Reptilia, 10.
Classification, 101.
Colour variation, 115.
COMMON LIZARD—
  Anatomy, 14-23.
  Classification, 101.
  Colours, 47, 48, 50, 93.
  Description, 47-50.
  Disposition, 52, 53.
  Distribution, 44-47.
  Feeding, 52.
  Food, 52, 53.
  Habits, 51.
  Haunts, 50.
  Head scales, 92.
  Hibernation, 40, 41.

COMMON LIZARD—*continued*.
  Length, 48.
  Movements, 51.
  Pores, 49.
  Reproduction, 53.
  Scaling, 48.
  Sexes, 93.
  Specific characters, 92.
  Synonyms, 53.
  Ventral scales, 48, 91, 92.
Coronella austriaca, 56.
COUNTY DISTRIBUTION—
  Aberdeen, 187.
  Aberdovey, 200, 201.
  Aberffraw, 201.
  Aberfoyle, 191, 192.
  Abergavenny, 173.
  Aberystwith, 200.
  Ailsa, 188, 189.
  Airth, 188.
  Alcester, 174.
  Anglesey, 180.
  Antrim, 193.
  Appleby, 184.
  Ard, 191.
  Argyll, 188, 190, 191, 192.
  Arran, 189, 190.
  Arthur's Seat, 190.
  Averton, 178.

COUNTY DISTRIBUTION—*contd.*
Aviemore, 191, 192.
Awe, 191.
Ayr, 188.
Bala, 200, 201.
Bangor, 200.
Barmouth, 200.
Bavelaw, 192.
Bedford, 198.
Berks, 151.
Birkenhead, 180, 203.
Bostal Heath, 169, 197, 198.
Bournemouth, 196, 197.
Brecon, 199, 200.
Bristol, 159, 195.
Bucks, 197.
Burnham Beeches, 174.
Bute, 188.
Cappagh, 193.
Cardigan, 199, 200.
Carlisle, 184.
Carmarthen, 177.
Carnarvon, 200.
Carno, 200.
Castletown-Berehaven, 193.
Charnwood Forest, 178, 202.
Chat Moss, 203.
Chelmsford, 174, 197.
Chester, 180, 181, 202.
Chichester, 168.
Church Stretton, 199.
Cirencester, 172, 199.
Clevedon, 158.
Colwyn Bay, 201.
Conway, 200, 201.
Corfe Castle, 163, 166.
Cornwall, 195.
Corris, 200, 201.
Crockham Hill, 171, 197.
Cromdale, 192.
Cromer, 198.
Crowborough, 196.
Culbin Sands, 190.
Culm Valley, 159.
Cumberland, 184, 204.
Deganwy, 200.
Denbigh, 200.
Denny, 191.
Derbyshire, 181, 202.
Derwent, 183.

COUNTY DISTRIBUTION—*contd.*
Devon, 159, 195.
Dorset, 163–166, 196, 197.
Doune, 191.
Dumbarton, 188.
Dunmore, 188.
Dunoon, 189.
Durham, 183, 184, 203, 204.
East Lowlands, 155.
Edinburgh, 191.
English Divisions, 145.
Essex, 170, 171, 197, 198.
Ewyas Harold, 173.
Falmouth, 167, 194.
Farnham, 151, 198.
Fernsham, 170.
Ffestiniog, 201.
Flat Holm, 177.
Forden, 200, 201.
Forest of Dean, 199.
Fowey, 195.
Garway, 173.
Glamorgan, 199.
Glastonbury, 158.
Glen of the Downs, 193.
Gloucester, 151, 159, 172, 198, 199.
Gosport, 161.
Graig Hill, 173.
Graigue, 193.
Gravesend, 198.
Hampshire, 162, 196.
Hanwell, 171, 197.
Harris, 188.
Hartlebury, 174, 175, 199.
Hayes, 170, 198.
Hayling Island, 162.
Hebrides, 190.
Hereford, 151, 152, 173, 199.
Herts, 197.
Highlands, 186.
Hindhead, 170.
Holyhead, 201, 202.
Humber, 154.
Hunts, 198.
Ireland, 148, 155, 156, 193, 194.
Isle of Man, 146, 154, 204.
Isle of Wight, 196.
Iver, 197.

INDEX

COUNTY DISTRIBUTION—*contd.*
Kent, 169, 197.
Kentchurch, 173.
Kerry, 193.
Killarney, 193.
Knockbolt, 197.
Knutsford, 202.
Lakes Province, 184, 185.
Lancashire, 181, 184.
Leicester, 178, 202.
Leighton, 200.
Lewis, 188.
Limpsfield, 197.
Lincoln, 179, 202.
Liverpool, 203.
Llanbedr, 201.
Llanberis, 201.
Llandegfan, 201, 202.
Llanerfyl, 201.
Llangollen, 201.
Llanrwst, 201.
Llansilin, 201.
Loch Tay, 187.
Meath, 193.
Menai Straits, 201, 202.
Mendip, 150, 158, 196.
Merioneth, 200, 201.
Mersey Province, 153, 179, 180, 202, 203.
Middlesex, 197.
Midlothian, 192.
Midsomer Norton, 159, 195.
Mitcham, 170.
Mold, 201.
Monmouth, 151, 173, 199.
Monnow Valley, 173, 199.
Montgomery, 200, 201.
Morecambe Bay, 184.
Moville, 193.
Mull, 190.
Nanhoron, 200, 201.
Newby Bridge, 202.
Newcastle-Emlyn, 199, 200.
New Forest, 197.
Newtown, 200, 201.
Norfolk, 171, 198.
Northampton, 145.
Northumberland, 185.
North Wales, 153, 178, 200, 201.

COUNTY DISTRIBUTION—*contd.*
Nottingham, 178.
Oban, 192.
Orkney, 188.
Orlestone, 197.
Ouse Province, 151, 171, 172, 198.
Overton, 179.
Oxford, 169.
Oxted, 197.
Painswick Hill, 172.
Parkstone, 163.
Peeblesshire, 192.
Pembroke, 167.
Pembroke Dock, 167.
Peninsula Province, 145, 150, 158, 195.
Penrhyn Deudraeth, 201.
Pentraeth, 201.
Perth, 187, 191, 192.
Petersfield, 196.
Pickering, 183.
Piperstown, 193.
Plumstead, 197.
Poole Heath, 196, 197.
Portishead, 168.
Portsmouth, 167.
Purbeck, 166.
Ragley, 174.
Renfrew, 188.
Rhosneigr, 202.
Ringwood, 196, 197.
Ripon, 183, 203.
Ross-shire, 186, 187.
Roundstone, 193.
Rum, 190.
Scarborough, 182, 203.
Scilly Isles, 168.
Scotland, 155, 186–192.
Severn Province, 151, 172–175, 199.
Sheire Common, 197.
Shetland, 188.
Shropshire, 152, 173, 199.
Somerset, 158, 195.
Southend, 171.
Southport, 179, 203.
South Wales, 177, 199, 200.
St. Asaph, 201.
Stafford, 173, 199.

COUNTY DISTRIBUTION—contd.
 Steep Holm, 177.
 Stirling, 187, 188, 191.
 Stornoway, 187.
 Stutland Heath, 197.
 Surrey, 170, 197, 198.
 Sussex, 162, 163, 196.
 Sutherland, 188.
 Tenbury, 174.
 Thames Province, 150, 169, 170, 197.
 Tilford, 198.
 Towyn, 200, 201.
 Trent Province, 178, 179, 202.
 Tyne Province, 183, 203.
 Ulverston, 185.
 Uppingham, 202.
 Wakerley Woods, 179.
 Wales, 176-178, 200-202.
 Wareham, 150.
 Wellington, 151.
 Welsh Newton, 199.
 Welshpool, 200, 201.
 West Lancashire, 185.
 Westmoreland, 184, 204.
 Weston, 180.
 Weymouth, 163, 196.
 Wilts, 166, 167, 196.
 Woodhall Moor, 179, 202.
 Worcester, 152, 174.
 Wrexham, 201.
 Wye Valley, 199.
 Wykeham High Moor, 182, 303.
 Wyre Forest, 152, 174, 199.
 Yorkshire, 182, 183, 203.

DESCRIPTION OF—
 Green Lizard, 72, 73.
 Sand Lizard, 61, 62.
 Slow-worm, 28-33.
 Viviparous Lizard, 47-50.
 Wall Lizard, 77.
DISTRIBUTION OF—
 Green Lizard, 69-72.
 Sand Lizard, 55-61.
 Slow-worm, 27, 28.
 Viviparous Lizard, 45-47.
 Wall Lizard, 77.
Diet, 34-36, 52, 65, 74, 78.
Digits, 17.

Disposition, 42, 43, 63-65.
Dissections, 108.
Distension of throat, 36.

EGGS, 12, 66, 75.
Endo-skeleton, 16.
Enemies of lizards, 41, 67, 74.
Eyelids, 11, 27.
Exo-skeleton, 15.

FEEDING, 20, 40, 51, 35.
Food, 23, 34, 35, 36, 52, 53, 65, 74, 78.

GAPING, 36.
Gironde, 74.
GREEN LIZARD—
 Anatomy, 14-23.
 Average length, 72.
 Classification, 101.
 Colour, 72.
 Description, 72.
 Distribution, 68-72.
 Eggs, 75.
 Enemies, 74.
 Food, 74.
 Habits, 73.
 Haunts, 73.
 Reproduction, 74.
 Size, 72.
 Specific characters, 95-97.
Gullet, 19, 74.

HABITAT, 45, 55, 69, 77.
Habits, 31, 51, 52, 63-65, 73, 74, 77-80.
Haunts, 31, 42, 73, 74.
Hibernation, 40, 41.
Head scales, 81, 84-102.
Heart, 19.

INFRA-LABIALS, 87.
Intestine, 12.
Ireland, 46, 148, 155, 193, 194.
Isle of Man, 154, 204.
 ,, Purbeck, 166.
 ,, Wight, 160, 196.
Italy, 97.

JAWS, 8, 20-23, 27, 34.

INDEX

Kidneys, 18.

Labials, 87.
Lacerta agilis, 55-67, 93-95.
,, *muralis*, 76-80, 97-100.
,, *viridis*, 68-75, 95-97.
,, *vivipara*, 44-54, 92, 93.
Lacertidæ, 78, 91.
Lacertilia, 8-14.
Lateral fold, 29.
Length, 30, 38, 48, 62, 72, 77.
Limbs, 11, 17, 128-141.
Liver, 18.
Locomotion, 51.
Loreal, 87, 88.
Lungs, 19.

Medulla, 19.
Motion, 51, 139.

Non-poisonous, 27.

Œsophagus, 18.
Olfactory, 19.
Ophidia, 27.
Optic lobes, 19.
Orders, 101.
Ovaries, 18.

Pairing, 74.
Palæontology, 5.
Pancreas, 18.
Physiology, 4.
Pineal body, 19, 43, 44.

Radius, 17.
Recurved teeth, 27.
Reproduction, 12.
Reptilia, 101.
Respiratory, 19.
Ribs, 16.
Rostral, 87.

Sand Lizard—
  Average length, 62.
  Classification, 101.
  Colour, 59, 61, 65, 66.
  Description, 61, 62.
  Disposition, 64, 65.
  Distribution, 55-61.

Sand Lizard—*continued*.
  Eggs, 63, 66.
  Enemies, 67.
  Food, 65.
  Habits, 63, 64.
  Haunts, 63.
  Hibernation, 41.
  Records of, 56.
  Reproduction, 66.
  Size, 62.
  Sloughing, 39, 40.
  Specific characters, 93-95.
Scaly lizard, 53.
Sloughing, 39, 52.
Slow-worm—
  Average length, 28, 29.
  Classification, 101.
  Colour, 33, 34.
  Description, 28-30.
  Disposition, 31.
  Dissections, 108-110.
  Distribution, 27, 28.
  Enemies, 32, 41.
  Food, 34-36.
  Habits, 31.
  Haunts, 31.
  Hibernation, 41.
  Limbs, 128-141.
  Movements, 33.
  Reproduction, 37.
  Size, 30.
  Sloughing, 39, 40.
  Specific characters, 90, 91.
  Tail, 32.
  Teeth, 29.
  Young, 38, 39.
Slugs, 34, 35.
Squamata, 101.
Swimming, 51.
Synonyms, 53.

Tail, 11, 15, 17, 29, 32, 62, 72, 73, 91, 92, 94, 96, 98, 102-114.
Tarsal, 17.
Teeth, 11, 18, 27, 61, 65.
Temporal, 85, 100.
Terminology, 84.
Testes, 18.
Thigh, 49.
Thorax, 16.

Time of birth, 38, 53.
Tongue, 11, 27.
Trachea, 19.
Trunk, 15, 17.
Types, 82, 83.

URINARY bladder, 18.

VENTRAL scales, 75.

WALES, 176, 200.
WALL LIZARD—
  Catching, 79, 80.
  Classification, 101.

WALL LIZARD—*continued.*
  Colour, 77.
  Description, 77.
  Distribution, 77, 98.
  Food, 79.
  Habits, 77.
  Haunts, 77, 78.
  Reproduction, 78.
  Size, 77.
  Specific characters, 97-100.
  Tail, 79.
  Variety, 78, 77.
Water, 51.
Windpipe, 19.

Crown 8vo, pp. xvi and 383, price 5s. net,

BRITISH SERPENTS.

By GERALD R. LEIGHTON, M.D., F.R.S.E.

A Concise Description of the Life-History of the Adder or Viper, the Ring Snake or Grass Snake, and the Smooth Snake, together with their Distribution in all the Counties.

The Lancet.—"Dr. Leighton is an expert, and any ordinary person who digests the book before us will have a greater knowledge of snakes than he ever had before."

Manchester City News.—'Dr. Gerald Leighton's book is the first really worthy treatise on the subject."

The Outlook.—"Those who would know all about English Snakes, their habits and distribution, cannot do better than read Dr. Leighton's book."

Morning Post.—"Dr. Leighton and his publishers may be congratulated on the production of a very fascinating and a very useful work."

With 50 Illustrations.

EDINBURGH AND LONDON:
WILLIAM BLACKWOOD & SONS.

.. The ..
Field Naturalist's Quarterly.

Edited by GERALD R. LEIGHTON, M.D., F.R.S.E.

THIS New Journal is devoted to all the subjects usually worked by Field Naturalist and kindred Societies. It is conducted from the point of view of the ordinary member of a field club, not for the specialist or advanced student.

"THE FIELD NATURALIST'S QUARTERLY" is issued in the months of February, May, August, and November, and deals with each subject as much as possible from the point of view of the season of issue: thus the first number of each year specially treats of animal and vegetable life in winter; the next issue is a spring number, and so on.

Each issue consists of about Ninety-six pages, demy 8vo, with Illustrations. The Annual Subscription is **10s.**, payable in advance.

Contributions and correspondence from Secretaries of Field Clubs, etc., should be addressed to the EDITOR, "Field Naturalist's Quarterly," 17 Hartington Place, Edinburgh.

SOME RECENT PRESS OPINIONS.

Westminster Gazette.—"The interesting character of this periodical continues to be well maintained. . . . A really valuable feature of the magazine to many readers is that devoted to British Field Zoology. It is to be hoped that members of field clubs and societies will give 'THE FIELD NATURALIST'S QUARTERLY' their hearty support. . . . Must be to all field naturalists an attractive periodical."

Lancet.—"Each succeeding issue of this interesting quarterly seems to show some improvement on that of its predecessor."

Outlook.—"The papers are well written by people who know what they are talking about. . . . We wish Dr. Leighton's Quarterly a long life and a prosperous one."

EDINBURGH: GEORGE A. MORTON, 42 GEORGE STREET.
LONDON: SIMPKIN, MARSHALL, & CO. LTD.

Mr. George A. Morton's
New Publications.

EDINBURGH: GEORGE A. MORTON, 42 George Street.
LONDON: SIMPKIN, MARSHALL, & CO. LTD.

The Keeper's Book.

A Practical Guide to the Duties of a Gamekeeper.

BY

P. JEFFREY MACKIE

AND

A. STODART WALKER

With Special Chapters by Lord DOUGLAS GRAHAM, Captain SHAW KENNEDY, Dr. REID, JOHN LAMB, P. D. MALLOCH, and TOM SPEEDY.

In One Volume, crown 8vo, **3s. 6d.** *net (postage, 4d.).*

Note.—Although the literature of Sport is large and comprehensive, till the present time no book has been prepared exclusively for the benefit of gamekeepers. "The Keeper's Book" is intended to serve as a *vade mecum* for the gamekeeper, dealing as it does with all the duties of a keeper by moor, covert, river, and forest. All important questions, such as the improvement of ground and stock, and the duties of a gamekeeper during both the close and the open season, will be fully dealt with in general by the authors, and in specific cases by well-known specialists. For instance, Lord Douglas Graham contributes the chapter on "Wildfowling," Captain Shaw Kennedy will deal with the duties of the Deer-stalker, Dr. Reid writes on the training and the working of Dogs, Mr. John Lamb, advocate, on "The Keeper and the Law," Tom Speedy on the elimination of Vermin, and P. D. Malloch discusses the functions of a keeper in River, Loch, and Burn.

Dedicated to Their Excellencies Lord and Lady Minto.

Curling in Canada
AND THE
United States.

BY THE REV. JOHN KERR,
M.A., F.R.S.E., F.S.A.Scot., Minister of Dirleton.

Ordinary Edition, Extra Crown 8vo, 500 pp., with about 400 Illustrations. Price **7s. 6d.** net (to be raised on publication to **10s.** net).

Edition de Luxe, Demy 8vo, on Art Paper. Impression limited to 250 copies, signed and numbered. Price **£1** net (to be raised on publication to **£1. 5s.** net).

This volume contains a complete account of the Tour of the Scottish Team of Curlers sent by the Royal Caledonian Curling Club to visit Canada and the United States in the winter 1902, and of the most enthusiastic reception everywhere met with by the team. The numerous illustrations in the volume include portraits of His Excellency the Governor-General of Canada, Lord Minto, and Her Excellency Lady Minto, and portraits, either separately or in groups, of the majority of curlers who were met on the tour, with illustrations of most of the covered rinks on which play took place, important buildings, scenery, etc. Alongside the account of the tour there is given a succinct statement as to the rise and progress of the royal and ancient game of curling at each important centre visited by the Scottish team, with reminiscences of famous players in the various districts.

A special chapter is devoted to the impressions which the various members of the Scottish team formed of Canada and its people, on their memorable and historic tour, while for the special benefit of Transatlantic curlers there is included in the volume an official description of the Curlers' Court and the mysteries of initiation so far as it is allowable to reveal the same.

From Journalist to Judge.

An Autobiography.

By FREDERIC CONDÉ WILLIAMS,

Judge of the Supreme Court of Mauritius; late Puisne Judge of the Supreme Court of Natal; formerly Judge of the Northern District Court, Jamaica; sometime Editor of the *Birmingham Daily Gazette*, and of the *Windsor Gazette and Eton College Journal*.

With Portrait. Crown 8vo, **6s.**

"Judge Williams tells some good stories."—*Bookman.*

"Contains the cream of an interesting and varied experience. . . . His racy stories, portraits, and *aperçus* are unencumbered with the slightest alloy of tediousness or triviality."—*Pall Mall Gazette.*

"Brightly recorded out of his varied experiences and observations in many parts of the world."—*Times.*

"An amusing and attractive piece of work. . . . His reminiscences of the Birmingham statesmen of his day are well worth reading."—*Sunday Sun.*

"A lively autobiography of a varied and interesting life."—*Daily News.*

"A racy and popular book of reminiscences written with unusual frankness and good humour."—*Glasgow Evening News.*

"Full of interesting reminiscences."—*Sussex Daily News.*

"Thoroughly interesting. . . . We have a series of thumb-nail sketches of Birmingham statesmen. . . . They are of a certain historical interest."—*Northern Whig.*

Recollections of James Martineau.

With some Letters from him and an Essay on his Religion.

BY THE REV. ALEXANDER H. CRAUFURD, M.A.,

Formerly Exhibitioner of Oriel College, Oxford;
Author of "Enigmas of the Spiritual Life," "Christian Instincts and Modern Doubt," etc.

With a Photogravure Portrait of Dr. MARTINEAU.

Crown 8vo, **3s. 6d.** net (postage, 3d.).

"It is indeed a winsome and fascinating personality that meets us in these pages. . . . Mr. Craufurd has much that is interesting to tell us of his friend's judgments on his more noted contemporaries. . . . Mr. Craufurd's pleasantly-written 'Recollections' has a place of its own as a supplement to the more formal and complete biography of his revered and venerable teacher."—*Scotsman.*

"Distinguished by sympathy, refinement of criticism, and considerable suggestiveness and insight. . . . Verdicts on books and men and movements are scattered through these interesting pages."—*Daily News.*

"A vivid picture of the man. . . . A just and high and true appreciation of one of the noblest and loftiest thinkers of the nineteenth century."—*Examiner.*

"It is a tribute of affection, and there is heart as well as head in it. By all means read this book."—*Expository Times.*

"A finely critical and appreciative bit of work. . . . Full of reverence for the saintly character of the man. . . . Undoubtedly of abiding interest and value."—*Aberdeen Free Press.*

"It shows the mind of James Martineau in a marked degree. . . . Full of striking and suggestive thought."—*St. Andrew.*

Second Edition, Revised.

In stiff covers, price **1s.** net (postage, **2d.**);
in cloth gilt, **1s. 6d.** net (postage, **2d.**).

The Care of Infants.
A Manual for Mothers and Nurses.

BY

SOPHIA JEX-BLAKE, M.D.,

Member of the Irish College of Physicians; late Dean of the Edinburgh
School of Medicine for Women; Lecturer on Midwifery for
the University of Edinburgh; late Senior Physician
to the Edinburgh Hospital for Women
and Children.

Opinions of the Press and of Medical Men on the First Edition.

Athenæum.—"We can most strongly recommend Dr. Sophia Jex-Blake's manual; it is an excellent work, and we should like to see a copy in every nursery."

The Literary World.—"Her directions are eminently practical—the book should obtain a wide circulation."

Nonconformist.—"A very valuable little manual."

Scotsman.—"An excellent little practical manual—a book which ought to have a place in every household."

Medical Press.—"Deserves to be read with care by young mothers, who will find much in it to assist them to rear strong and healthy offspring."

From Dr. G. W. Balfour, LL.D.—"I have to thank you for your excellent little book, every word of which I have read with great pleasure."

From Dr. Symes Thompson.—"Let me thank you for your book on the care of infants, which is exactly what has long been wanted."

From Sir Thomas Barlow, M.D.—"I consider it most sensible, and that it ought to be of great use."

From the late Dr. King Chambers.—"I am much obliged to you for a copy of your little volume. It is quite an incarnation of educated common sense."

From the late Dr. Octavius Sturges.—"I am charmed with your book about the infants, and hope it will spread far and wide for the lighting up of a very dark place."

Drinkers of Hemlock.
A Novel.
BY A. STODART WALKER,
Author of "The Struggle for Success," "The Poet of Modern Revolt," etc.

Crown 8vo, **6s.**

"Full of clever satire."—*Daily News.*

"Most interesting and entertaining."—*Vanity Fair.*

"Mr. Walker has abundantly proved his powers as a novelist."—*Glasgow Herald.*

Windfalls.
BY ROBERT AITKEN.
With a Frontispiece in Colour by JOHN HASSALL, R.I.

Crown 8vo, **6s.**

"A very remarkable volume.... We have read no more striking first book since Kipling's 'Plain Tales.'"—*World.*

"The best piece of fiction this week."—*Morning Advertiser.*

"Gives proof of a keen power of observation, and a sense of humour equally keen."—*To-Day.*

"Brimful of humorous incident and exciting adventure."—*Glasgow Herald.*

The Very Short Memory of
Mr. Joseph Scorer.
BY JOHN OXENHAM,
Author of "Barbe of Grand Bayou," "Bondman Free," "John of Gerisau," etc.

Price **1s.** net; cloth limp, **1s. 6d.** net.

"Amongst the rarest literary gifts is that of writing a good short story. John Oxenham possesses it in a marked degree.... Suddenly, towards the end, there is introduced an unexpected development that charms and delights the reader."—*Punch.*

"One of the best productions of its kind.... A shilling's worth of genuine fun."—*Pall Mall Gazette.*

CPSIA information can be obtained at www.ICGtesting.com
Printed in the USA
LVOW12*1224091213

364507LV00004B/67/P